DAY OF THE DEAD COLORING BOOK FOR GROWN-UPS

Dia De Los Muertos Themed Sugar Skull Coloring Pages for Adults

Mia Blackwood

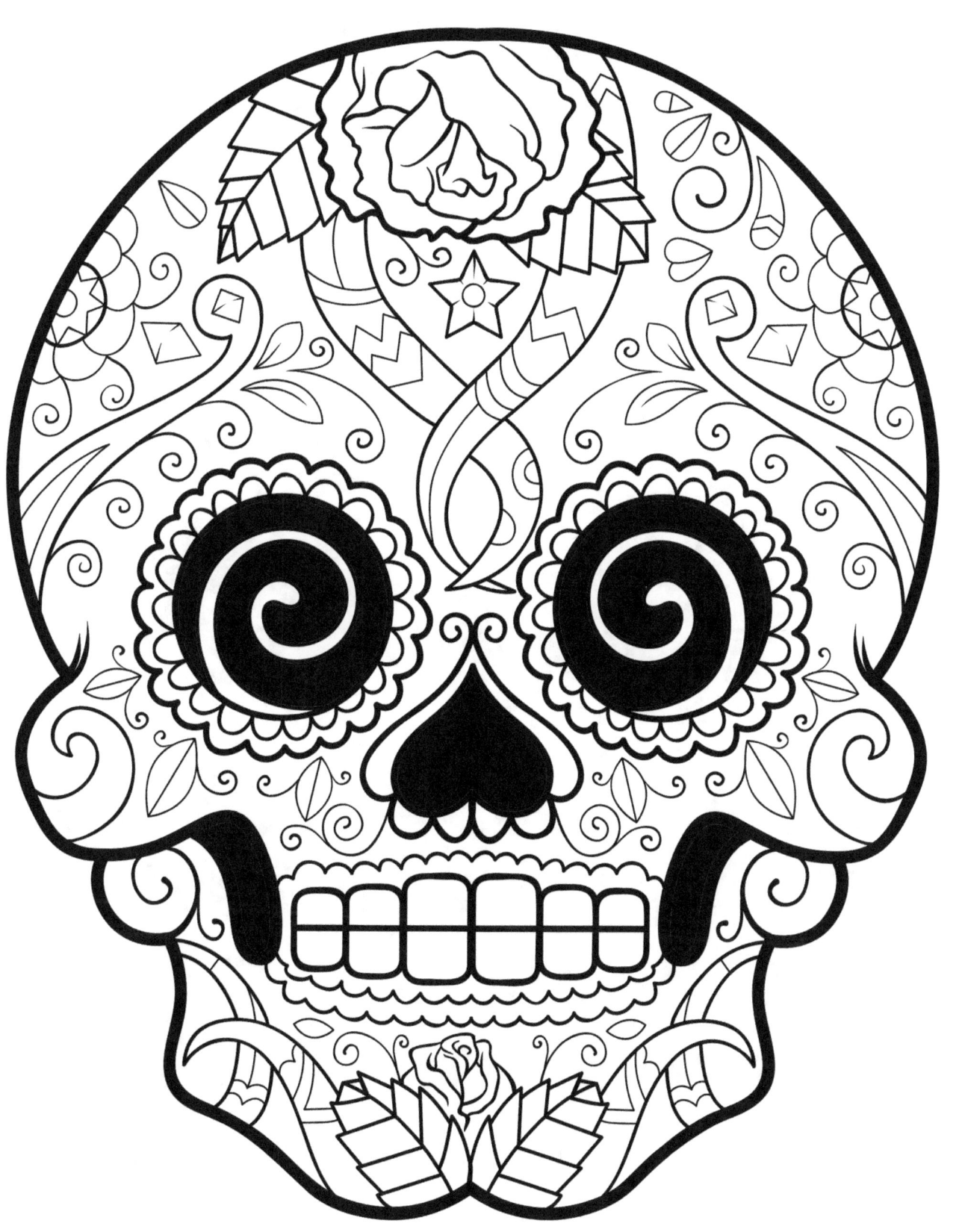

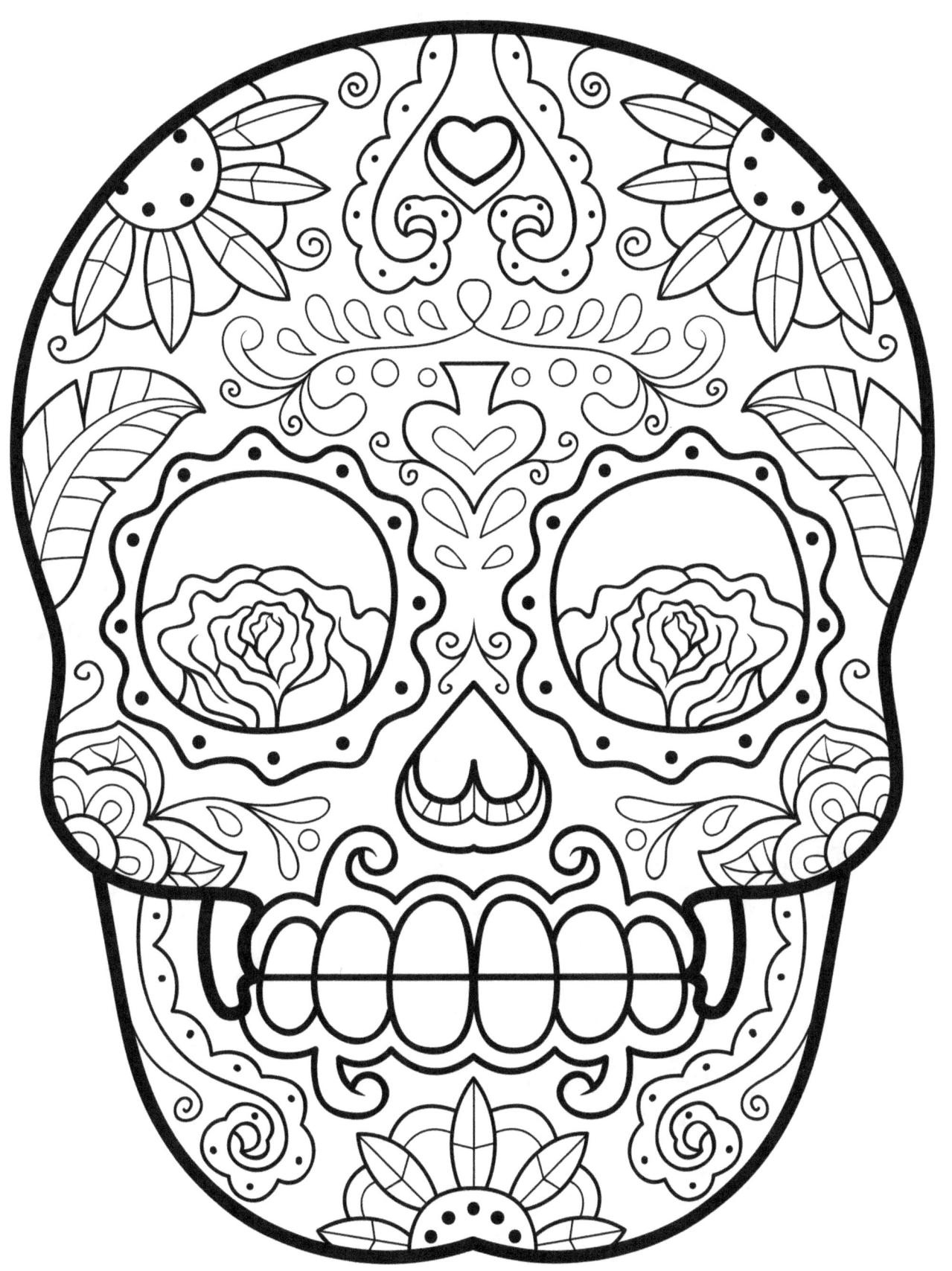

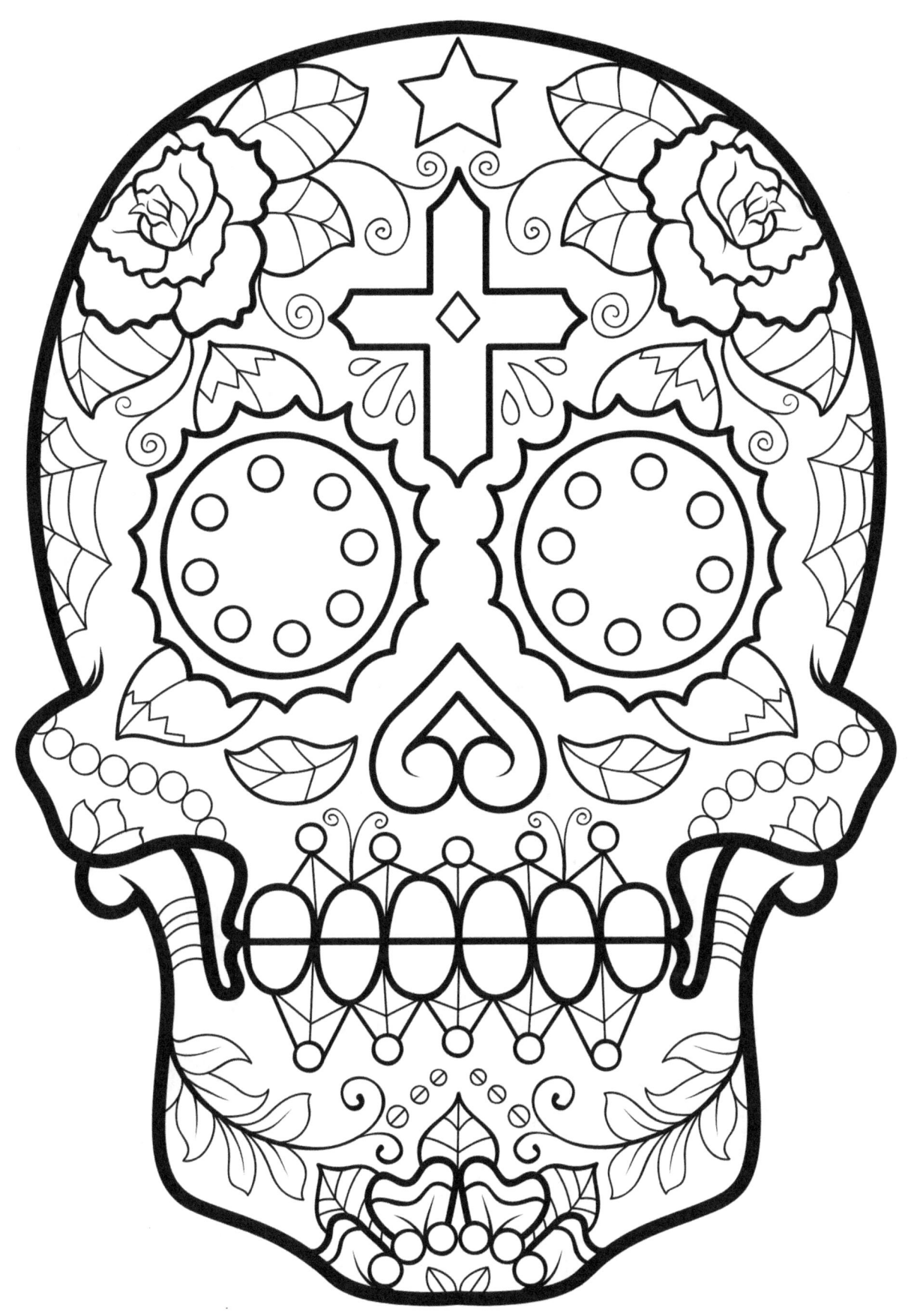

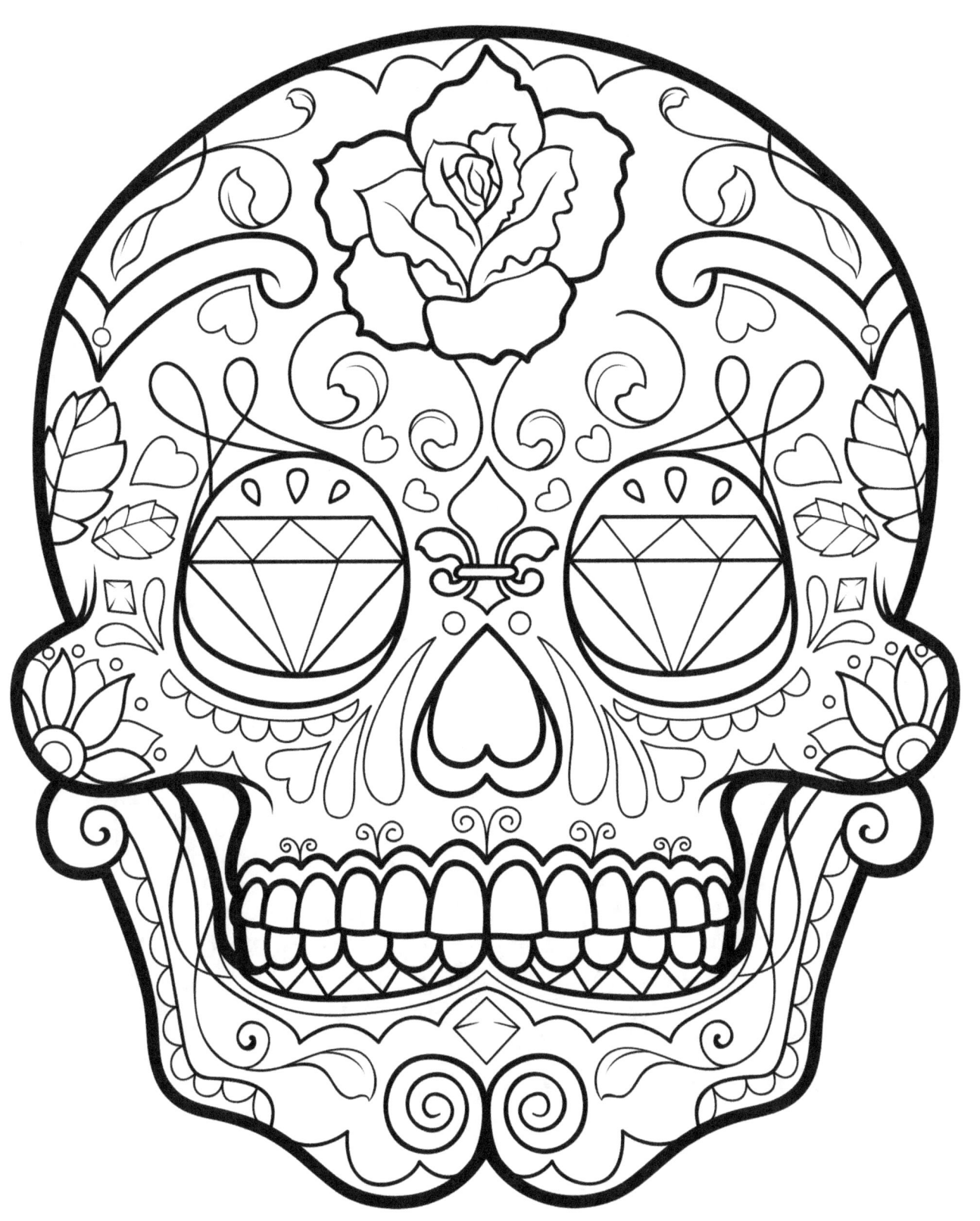

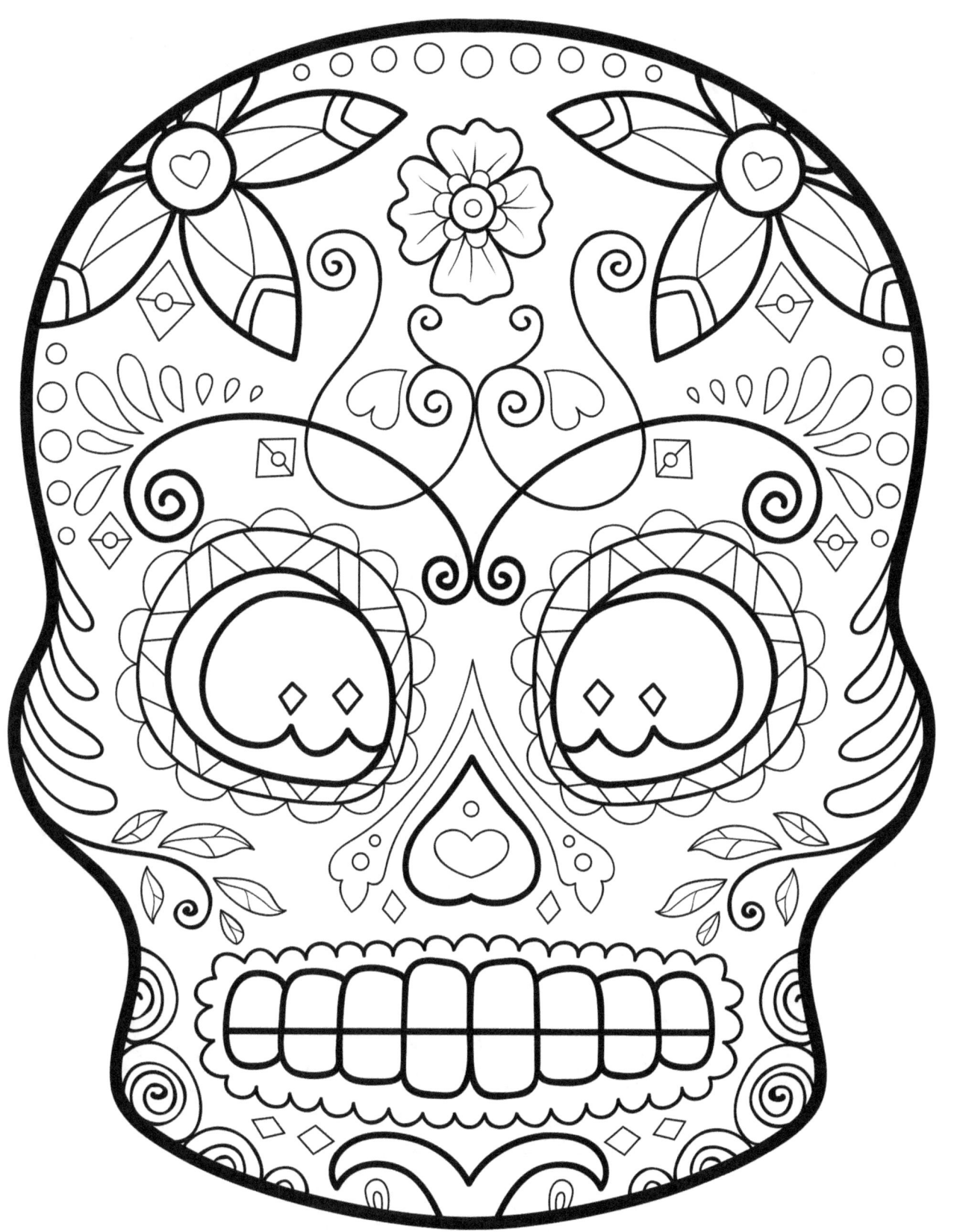

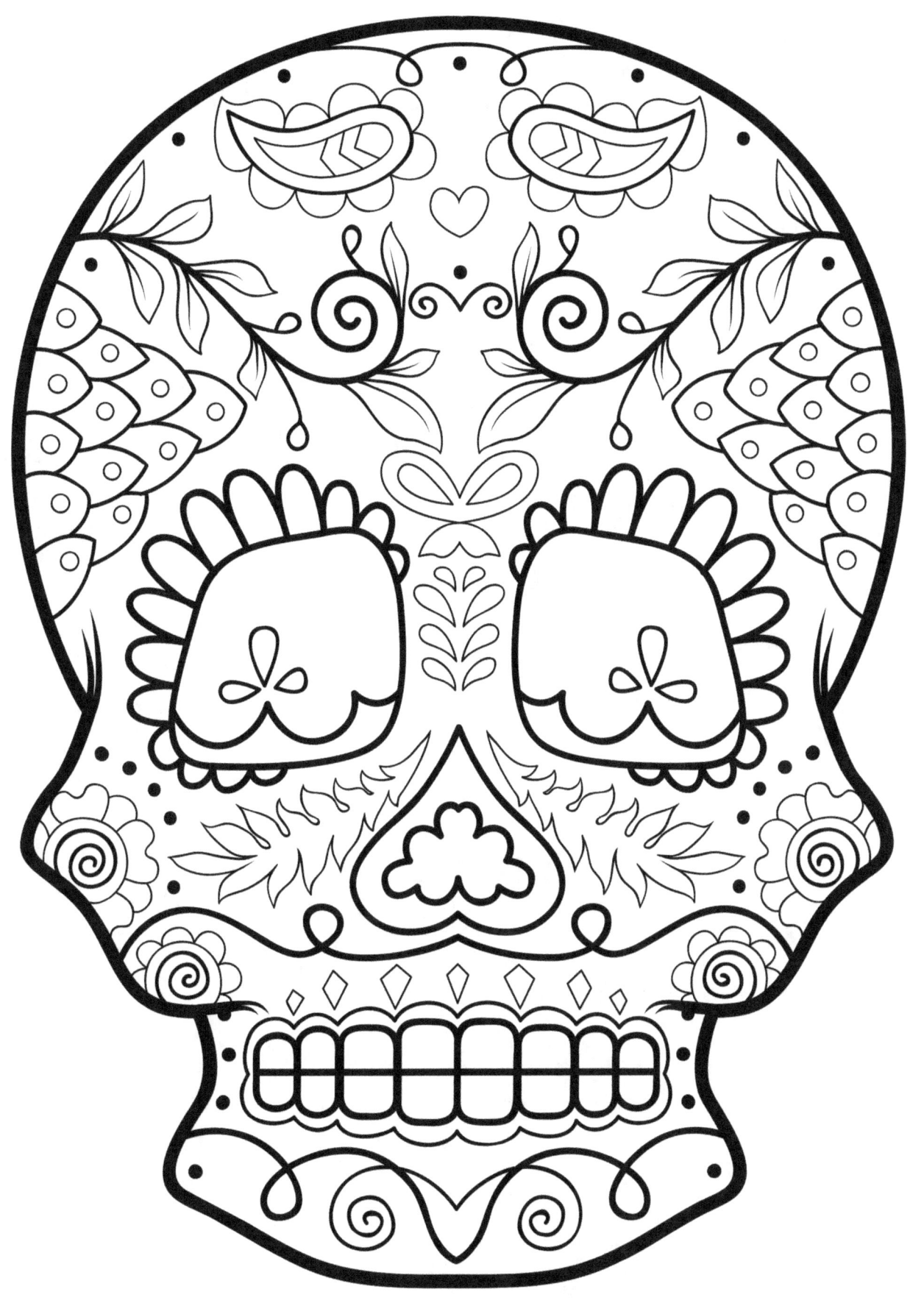

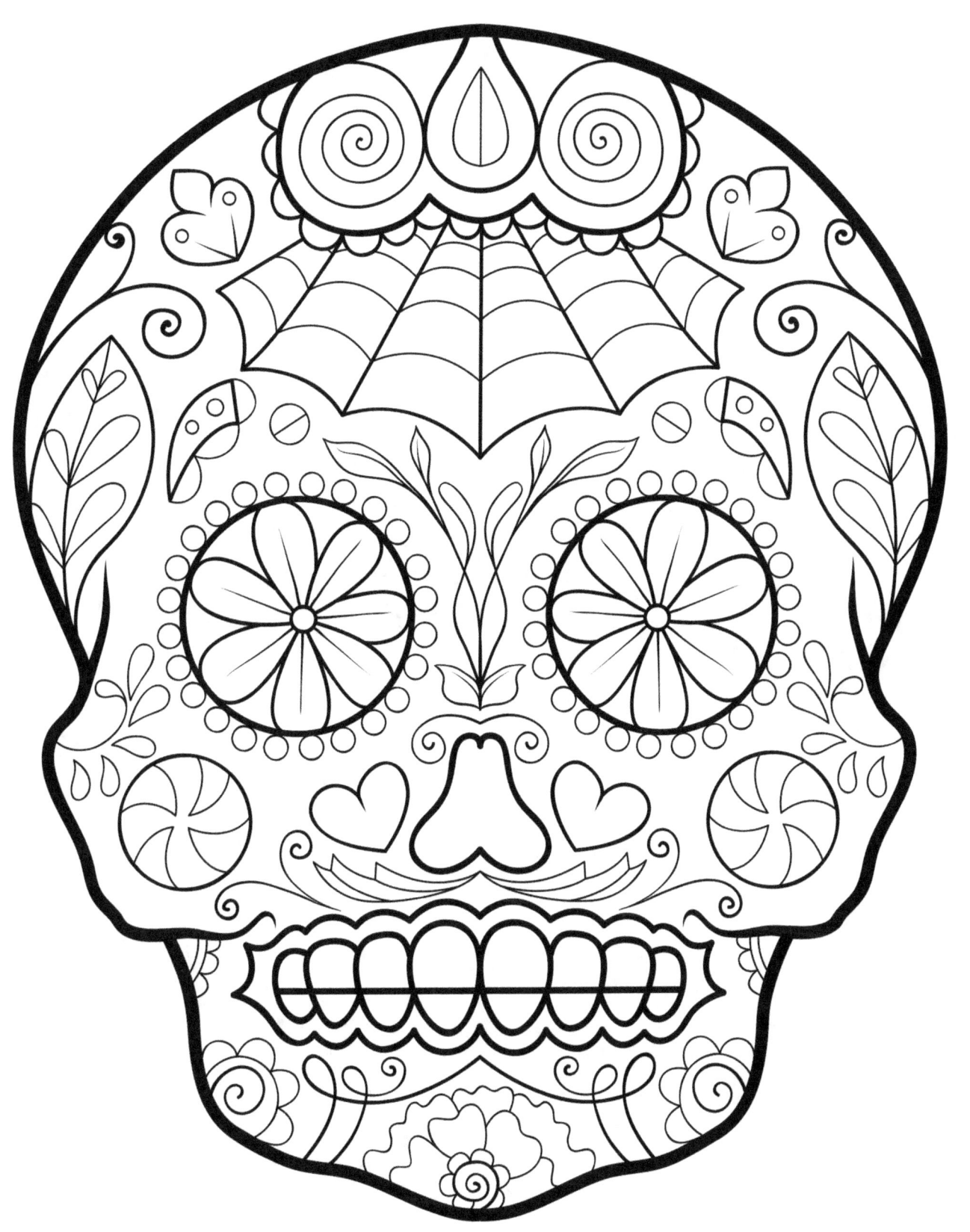

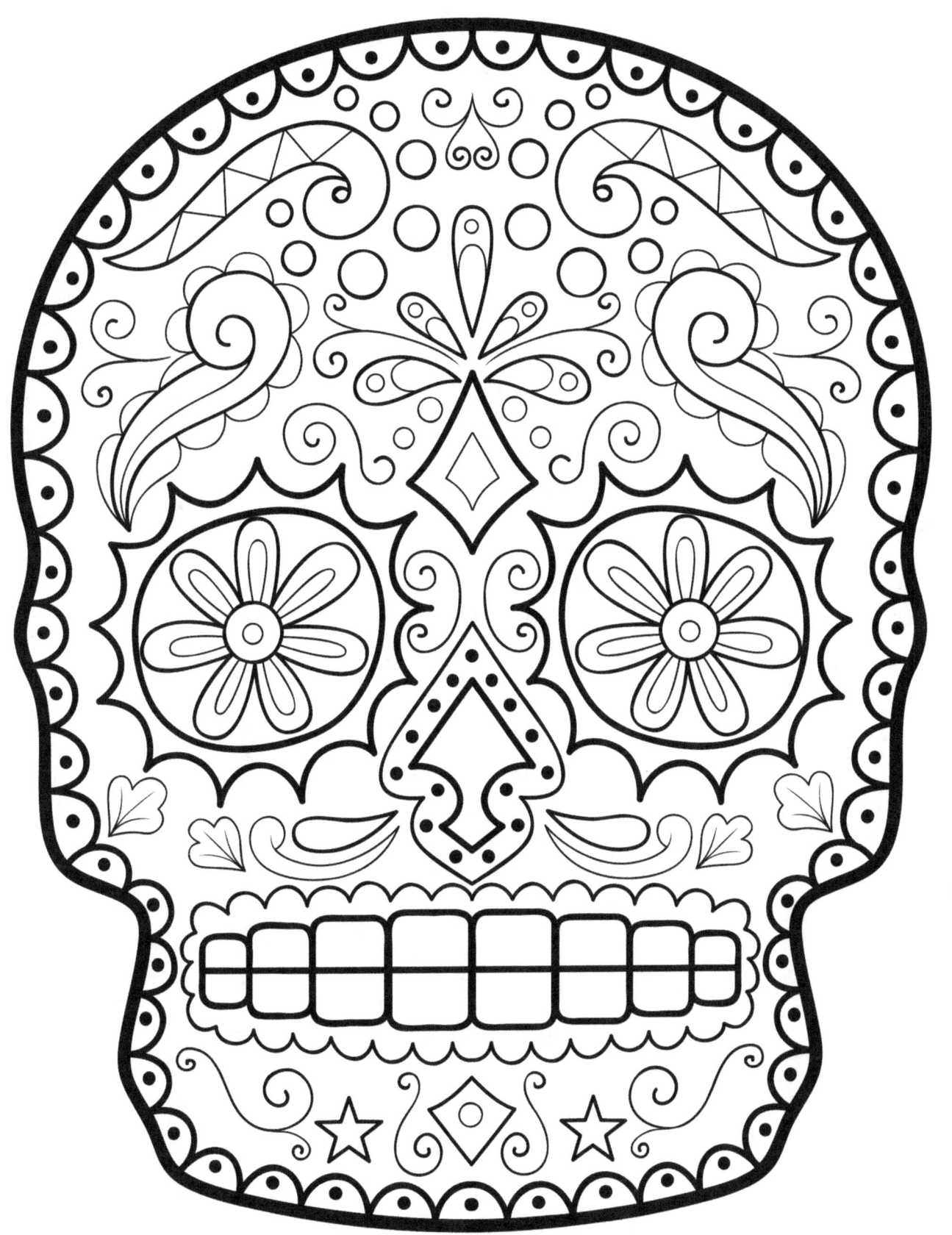

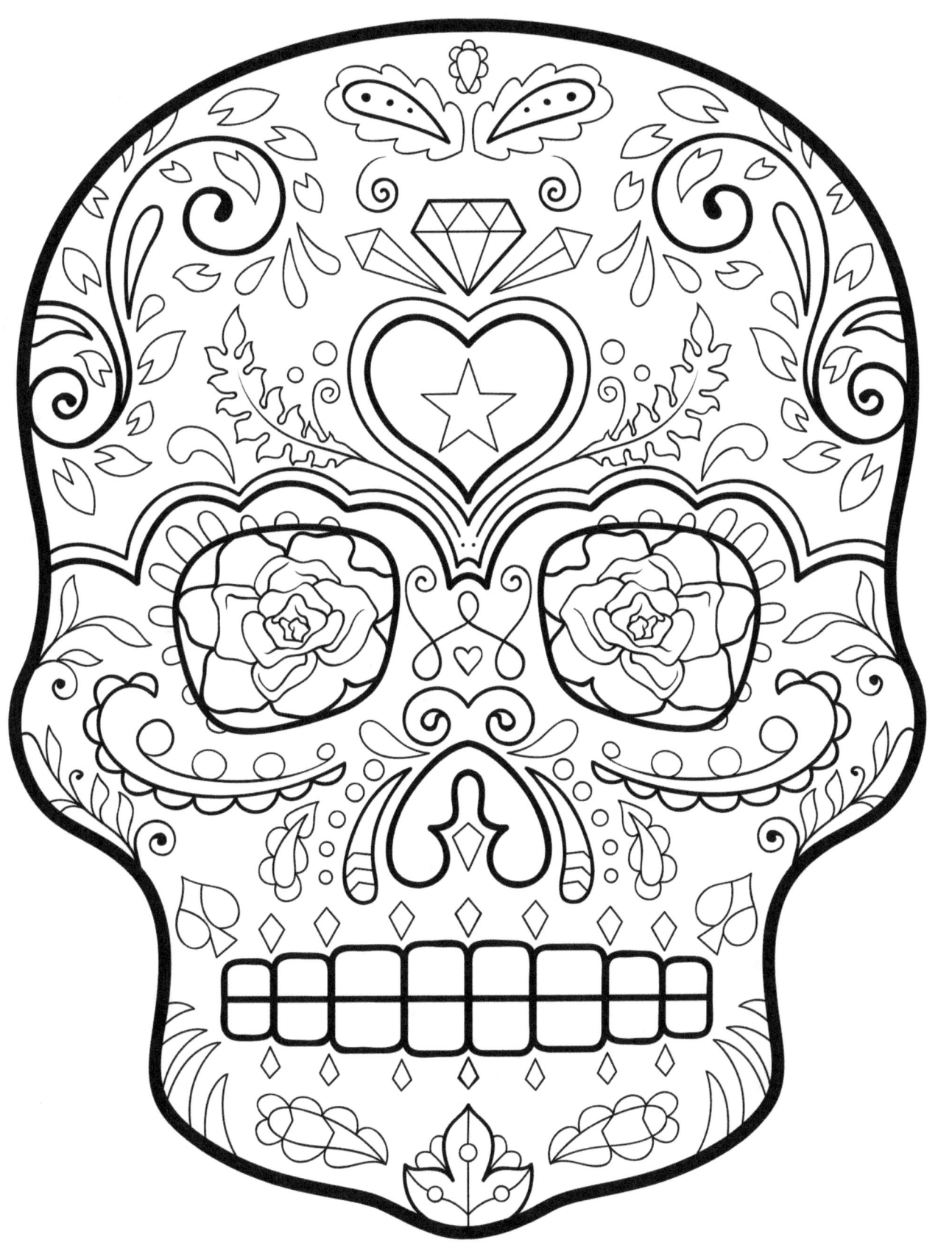

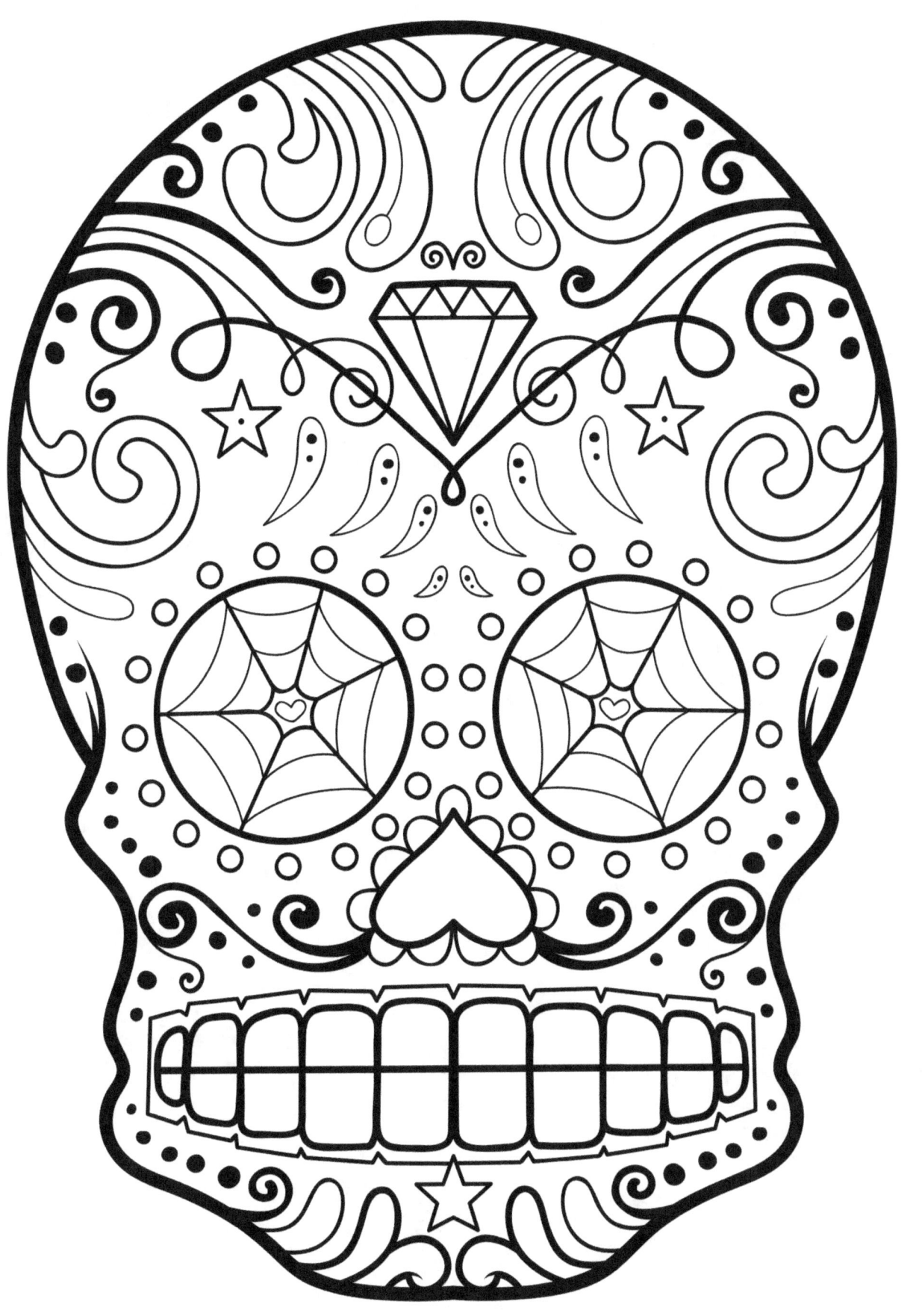

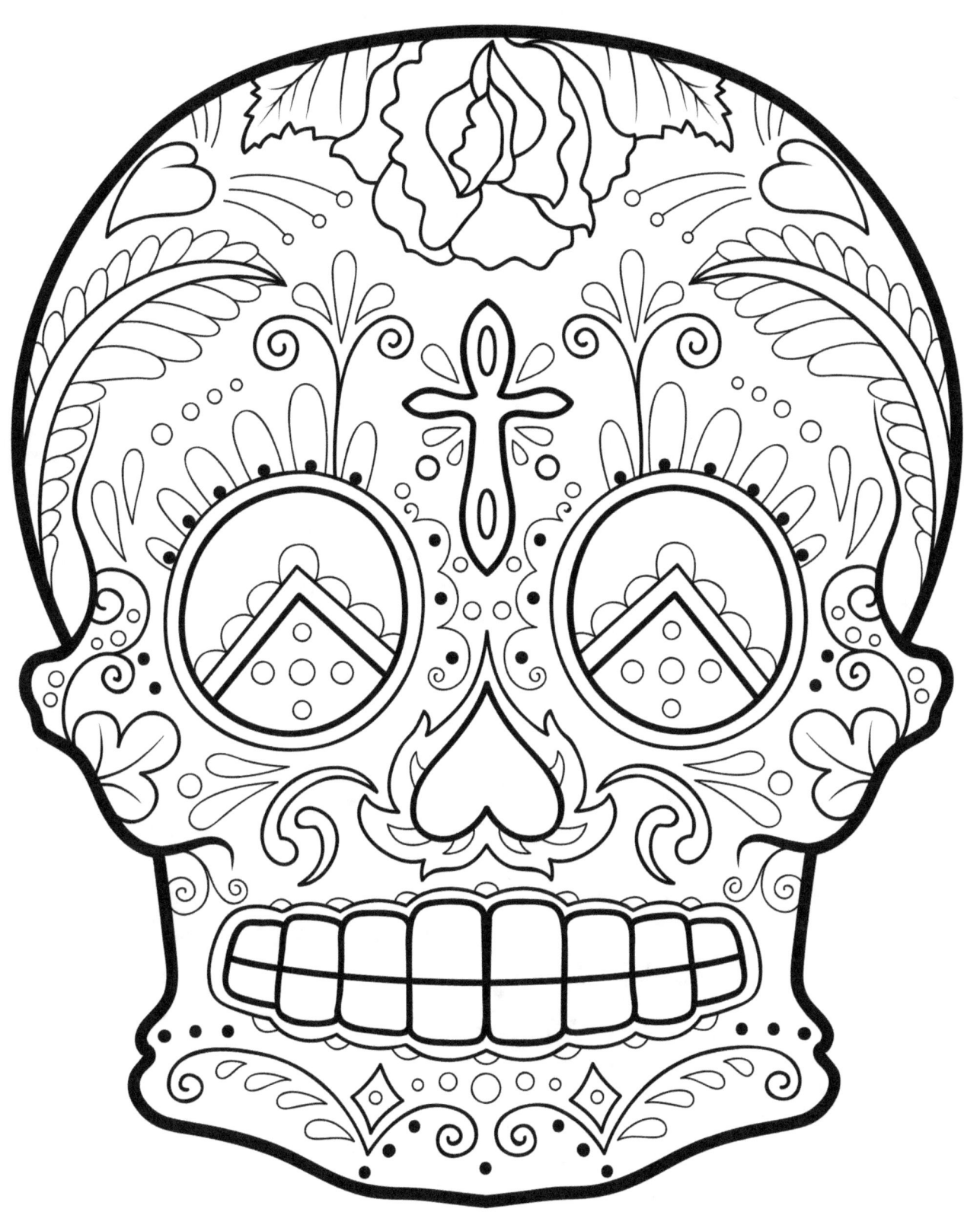

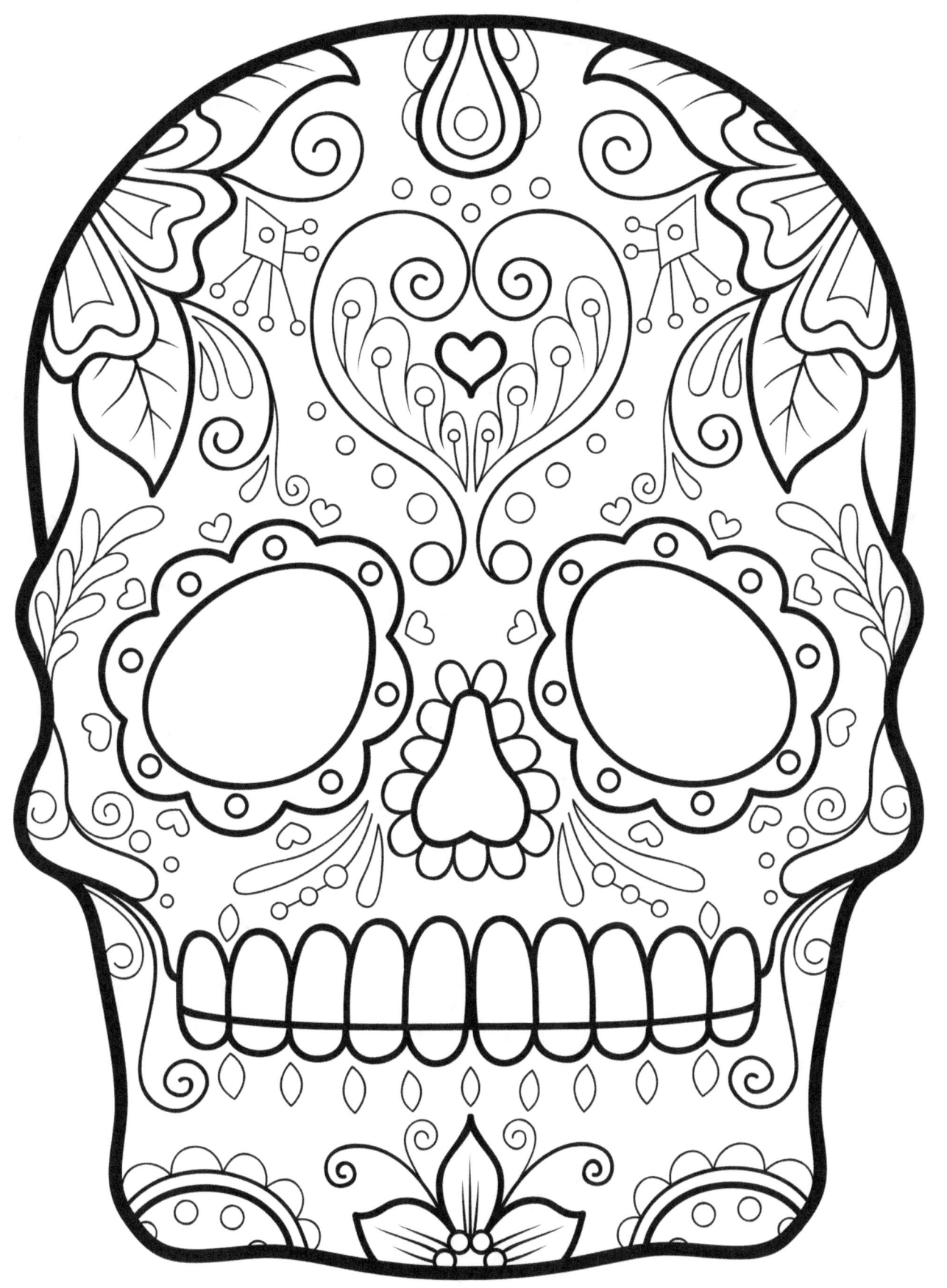

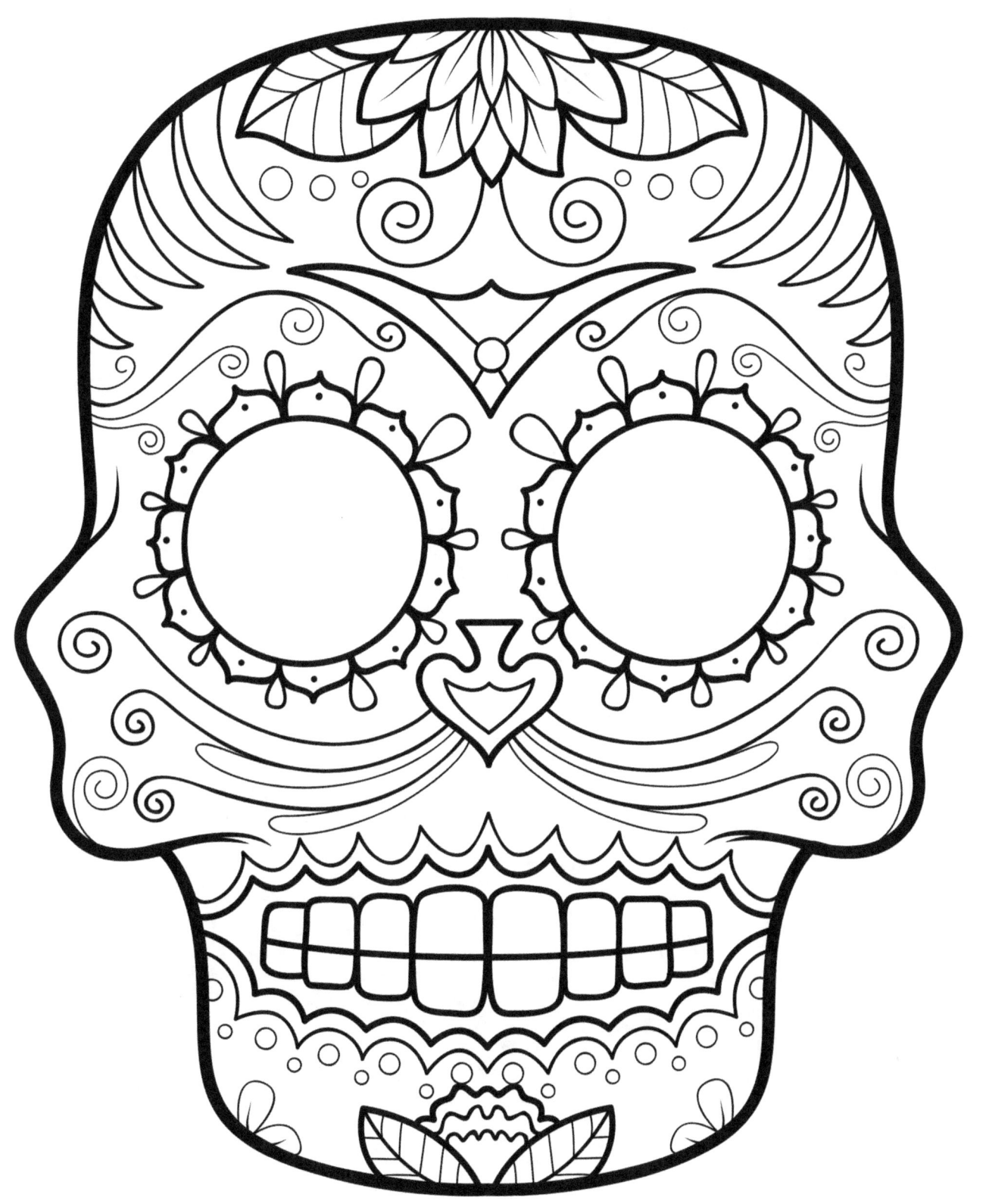

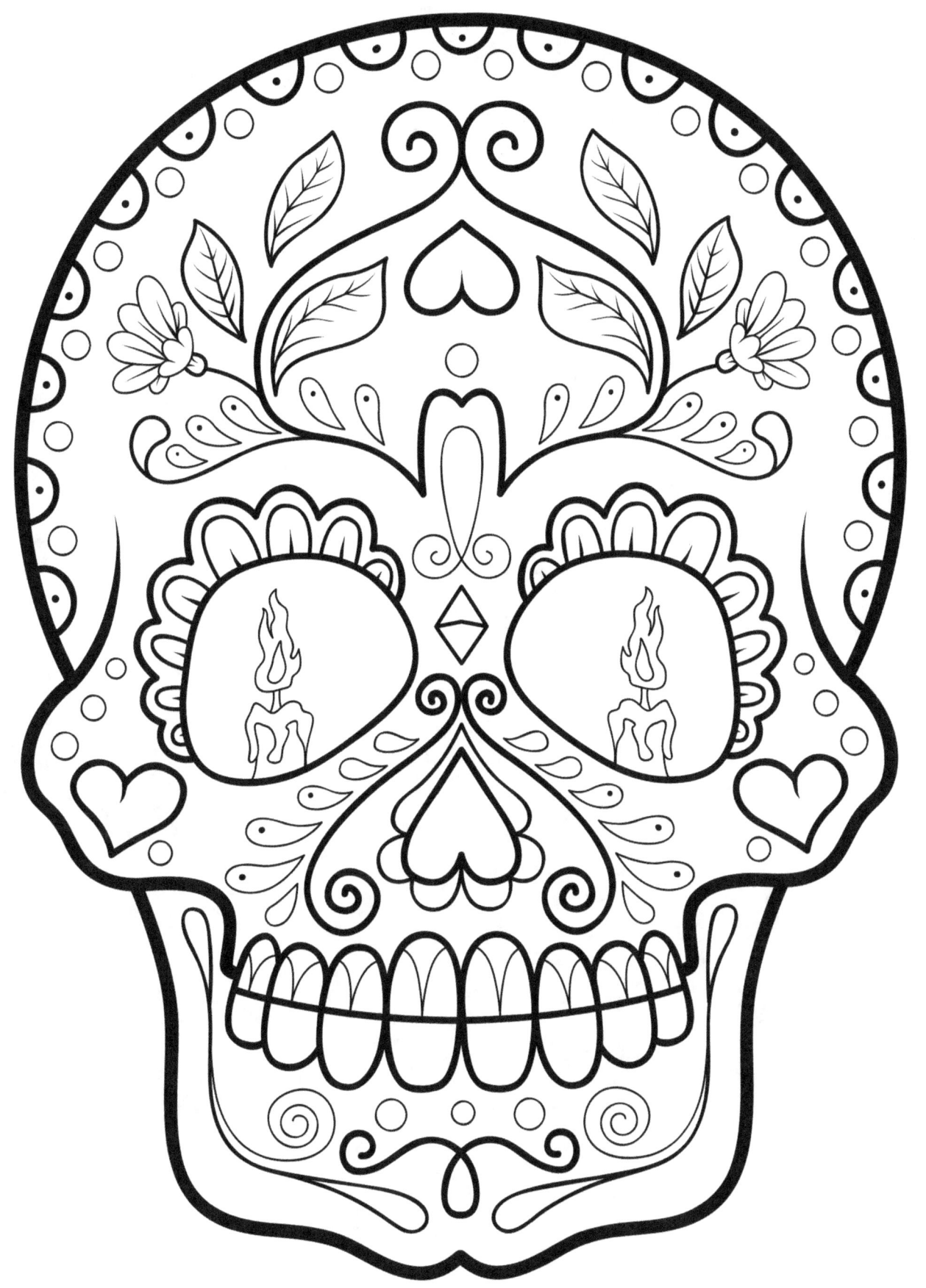

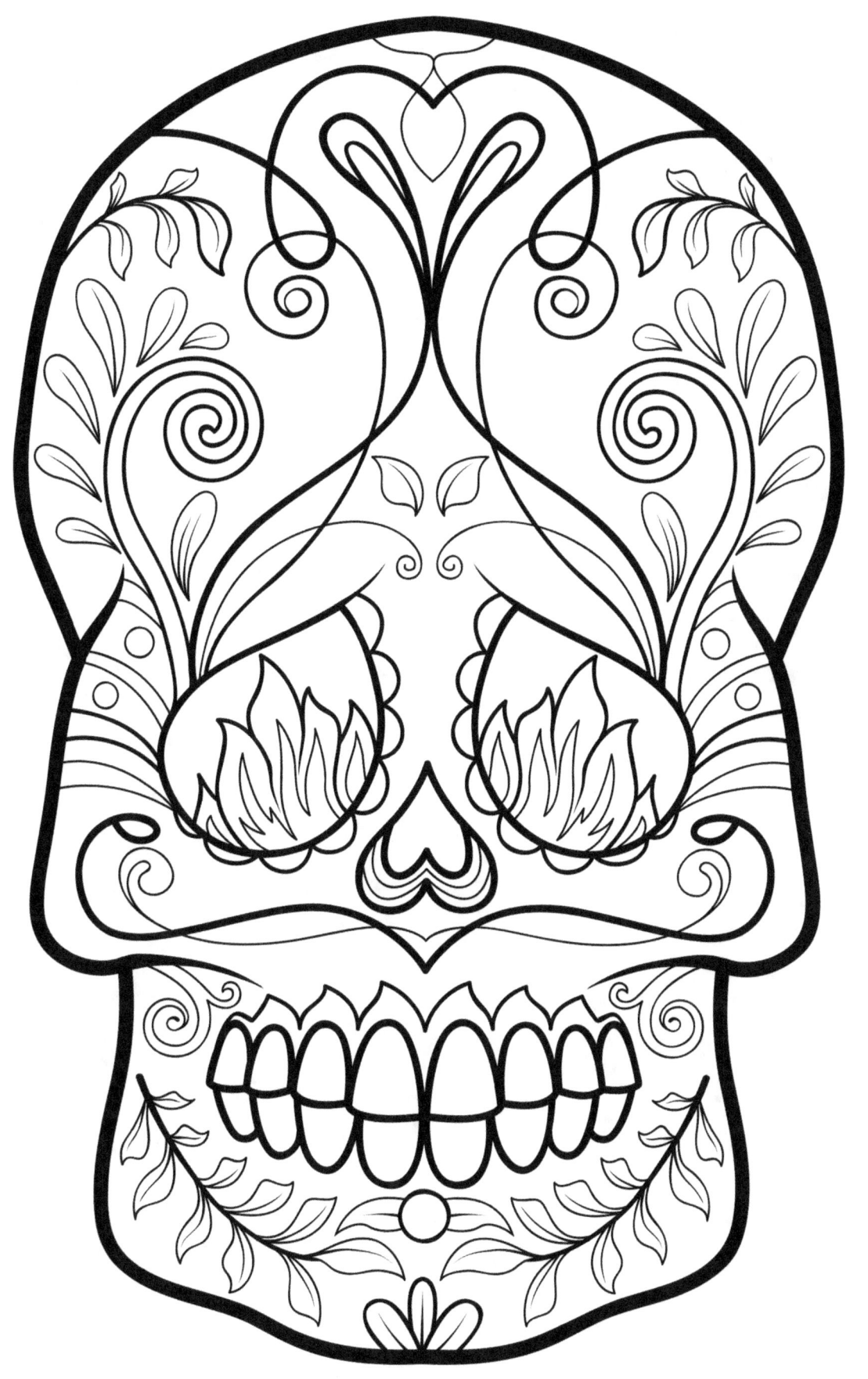

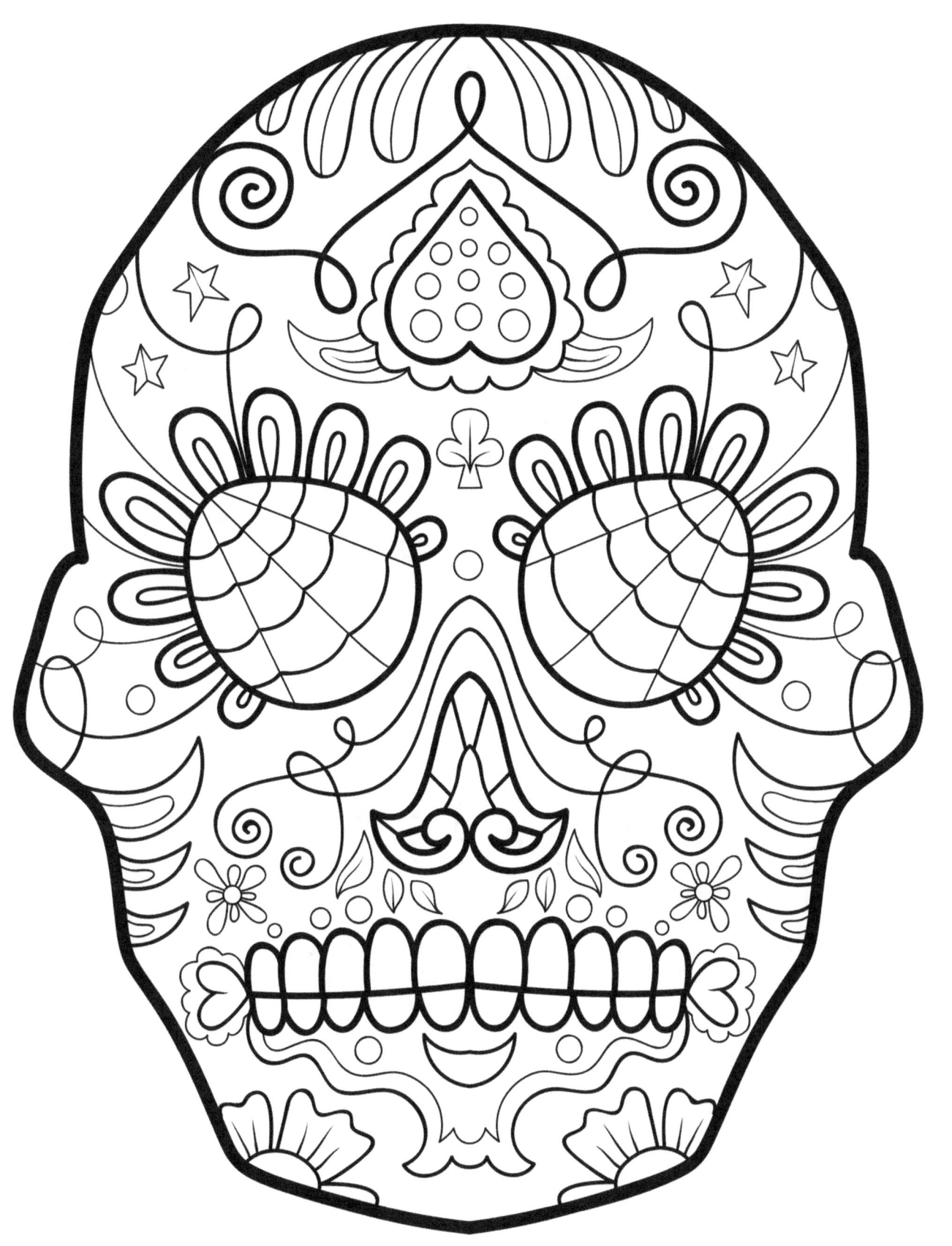

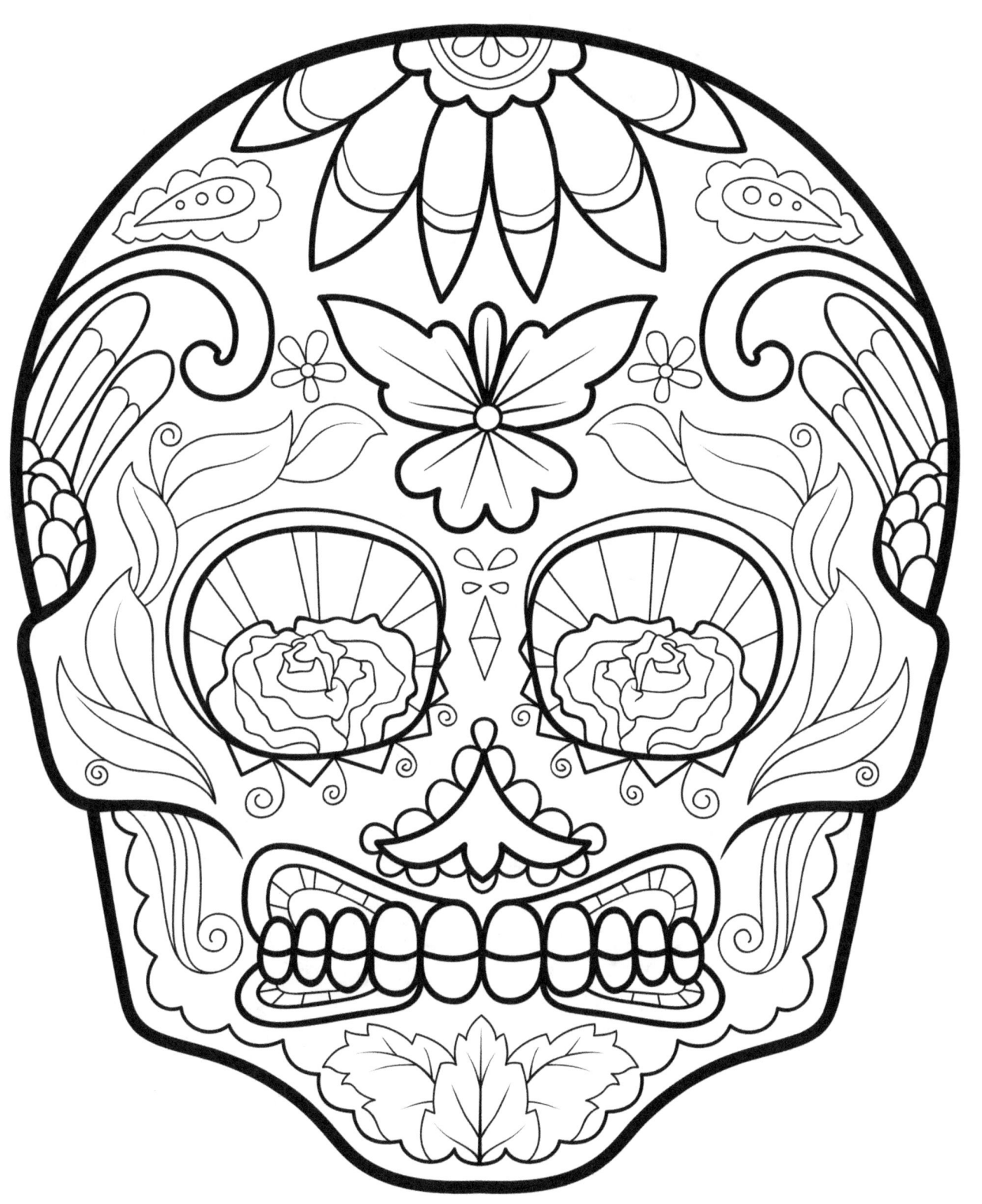

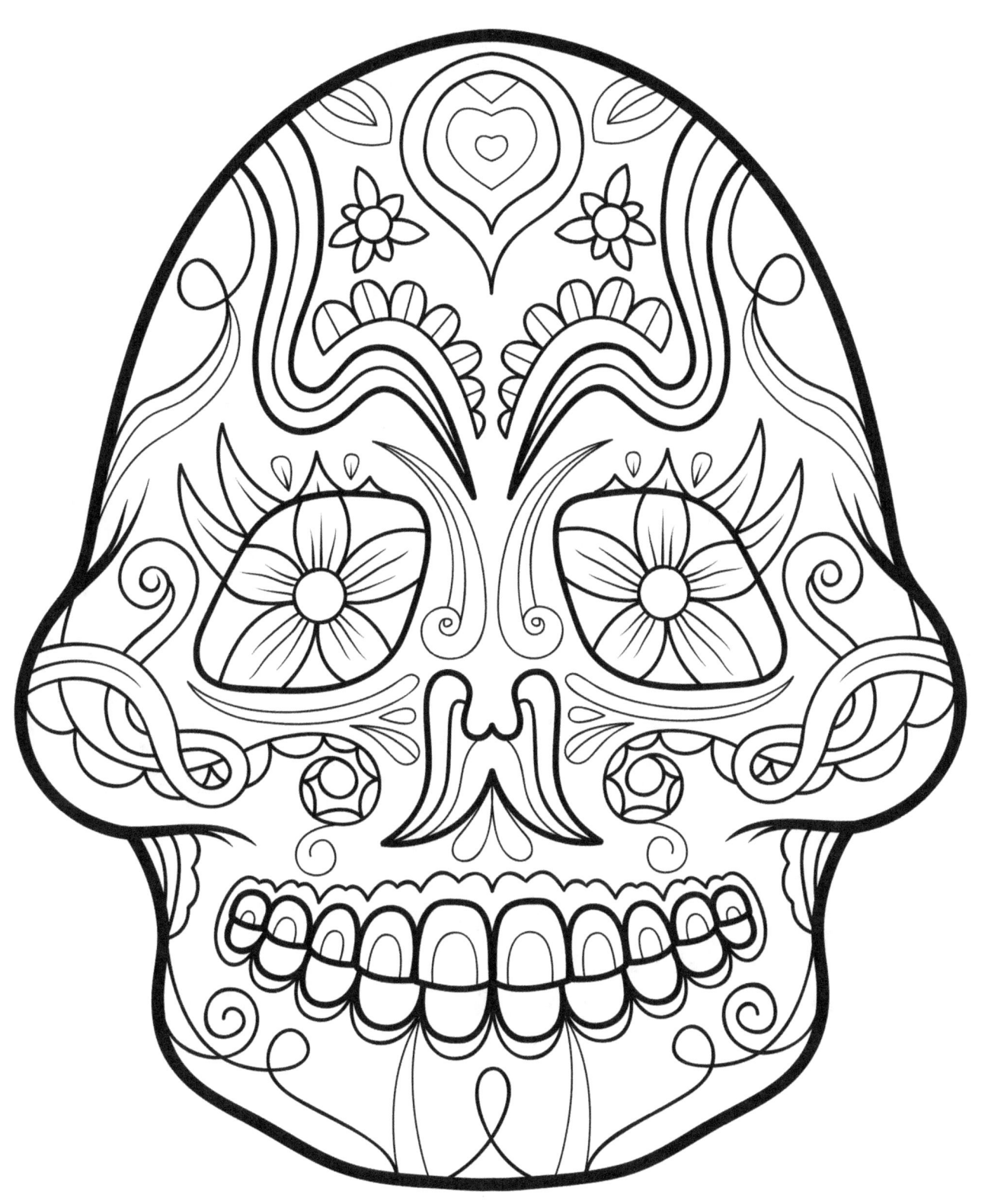

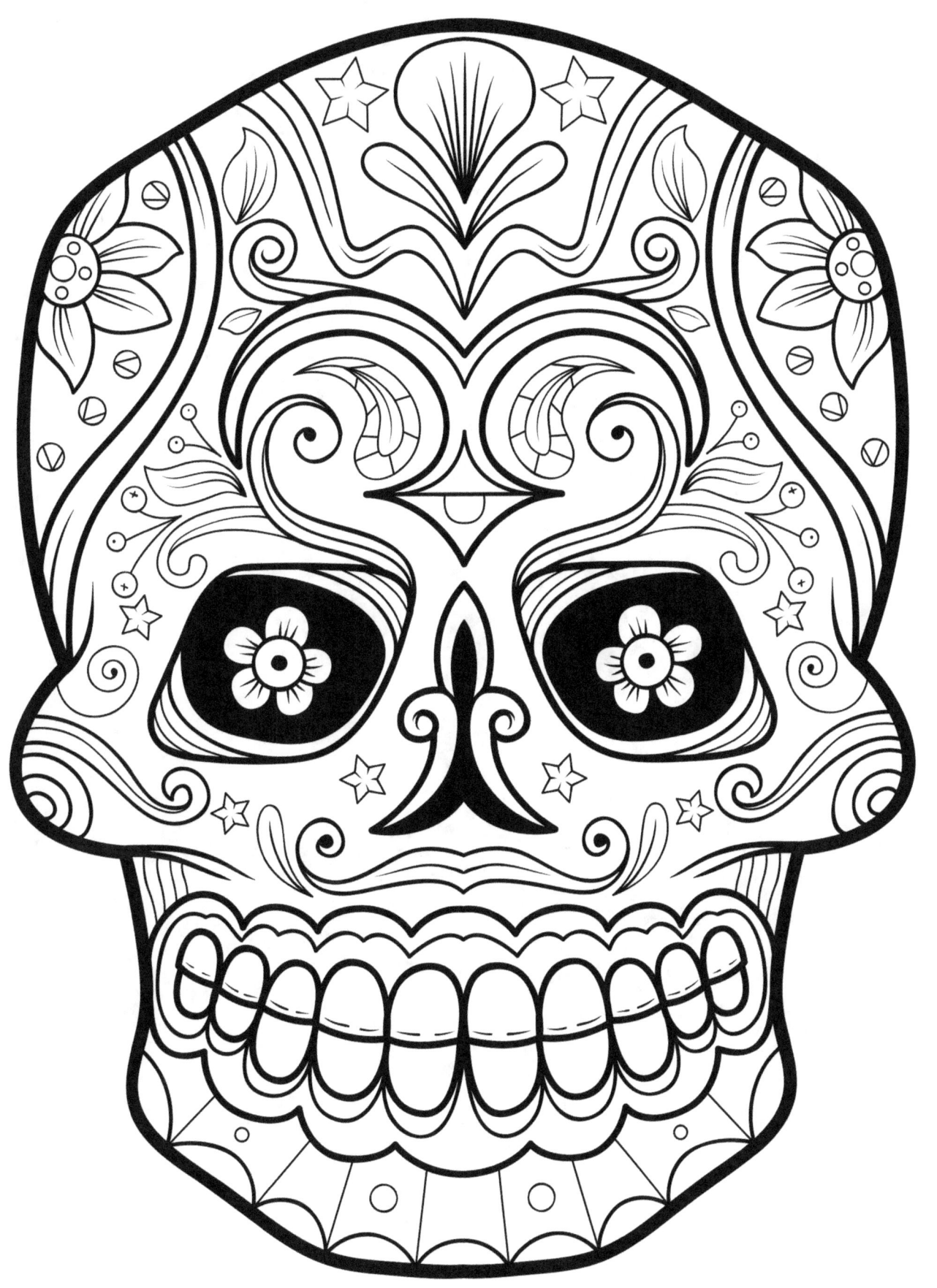

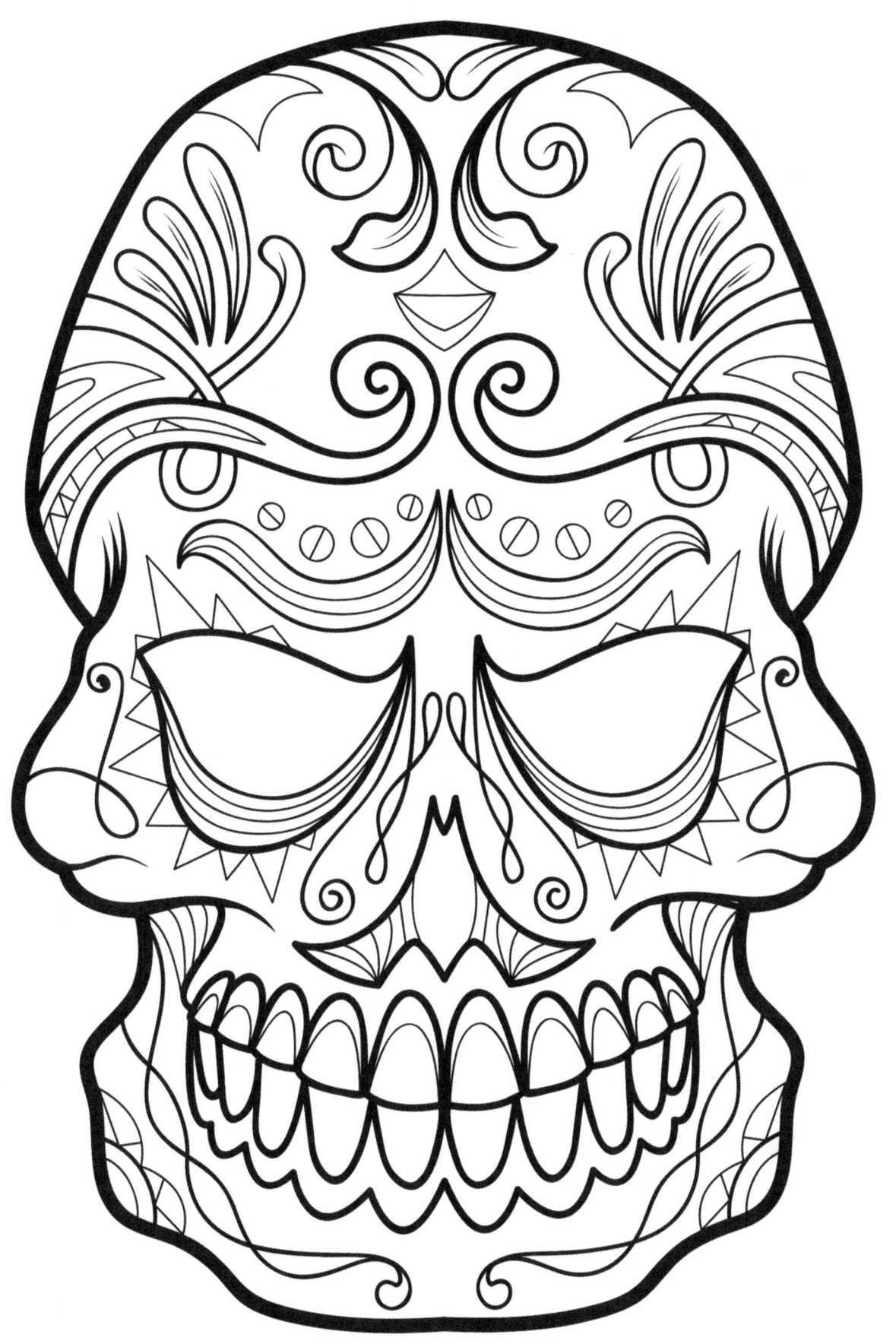

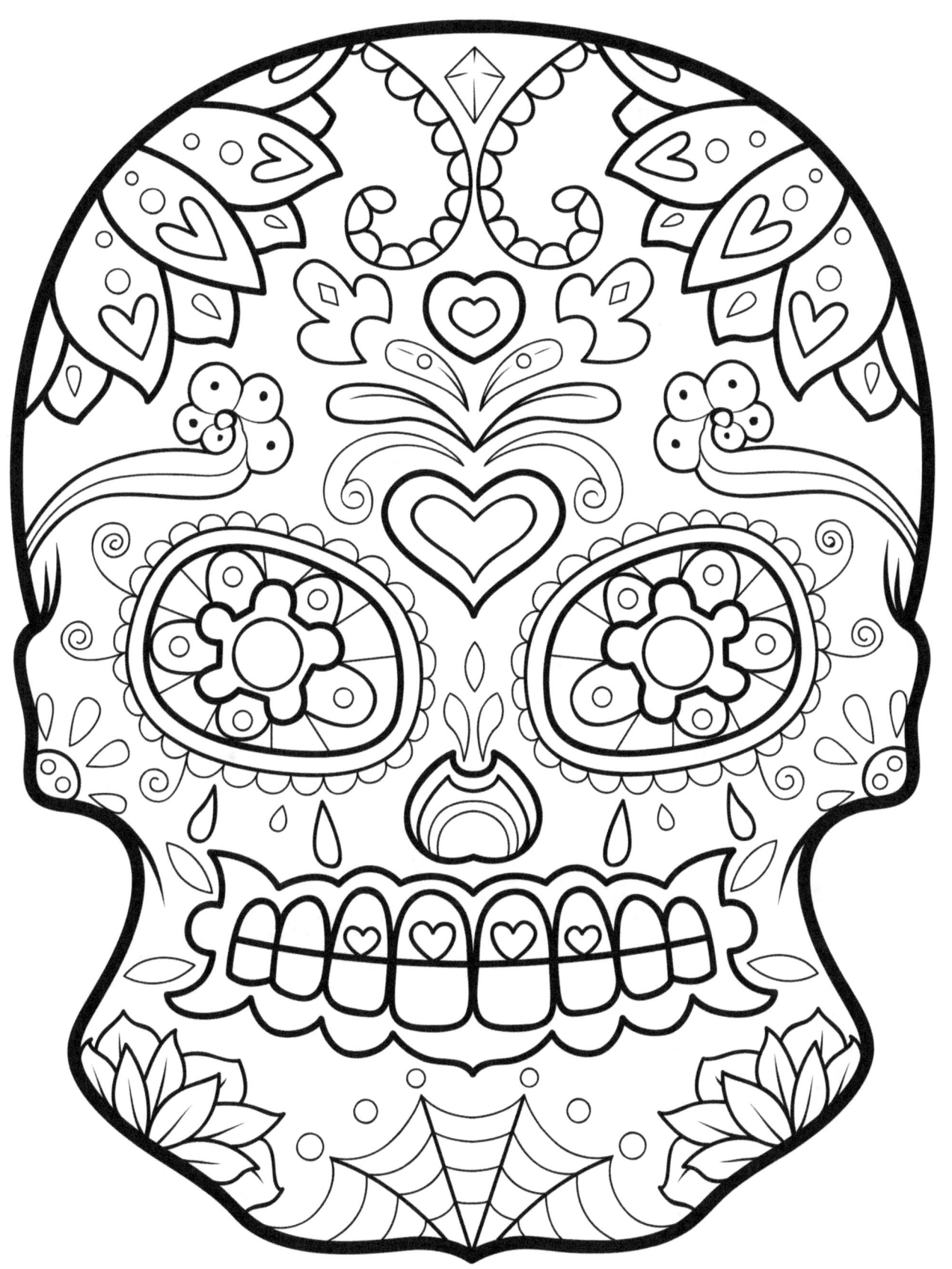

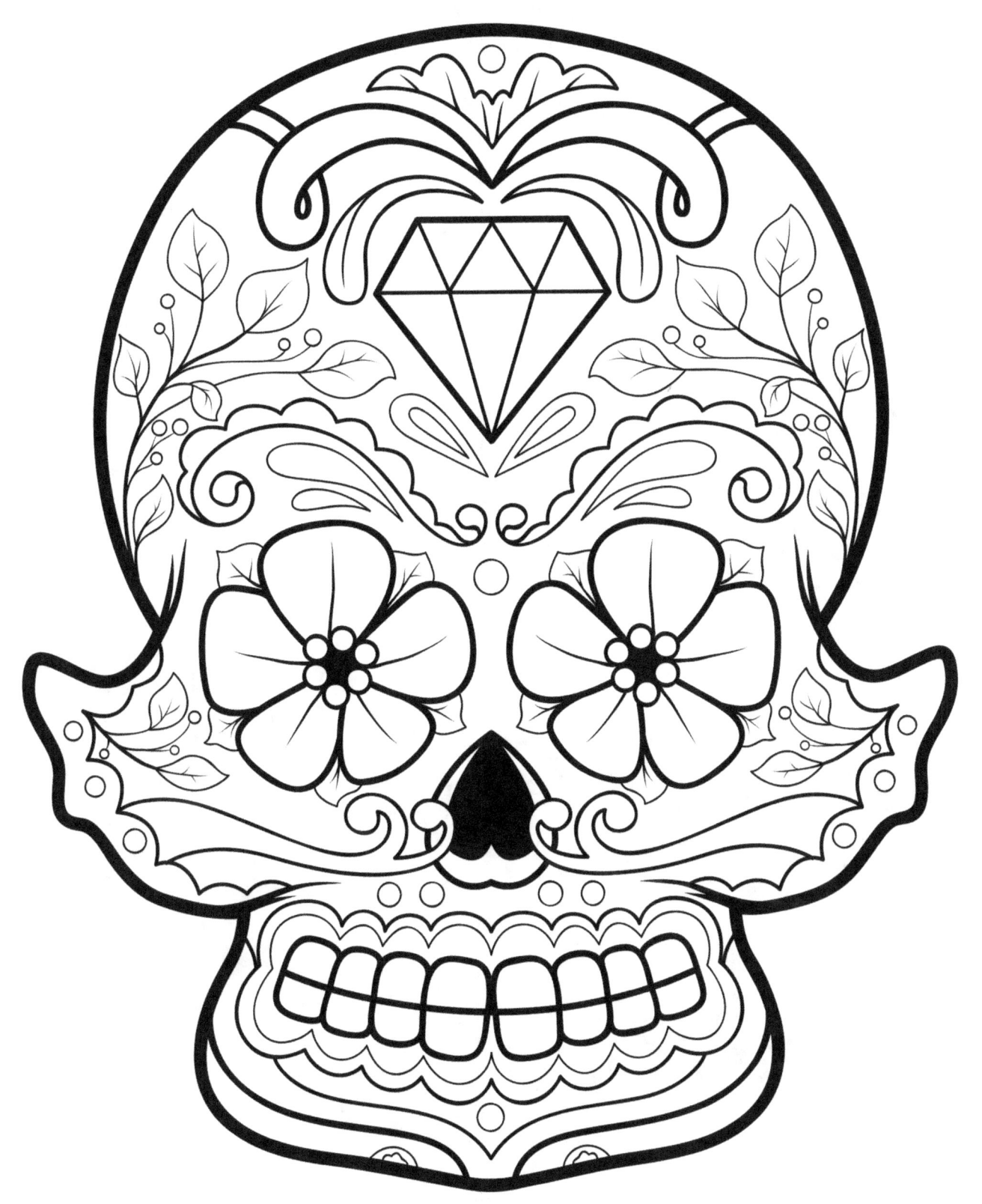

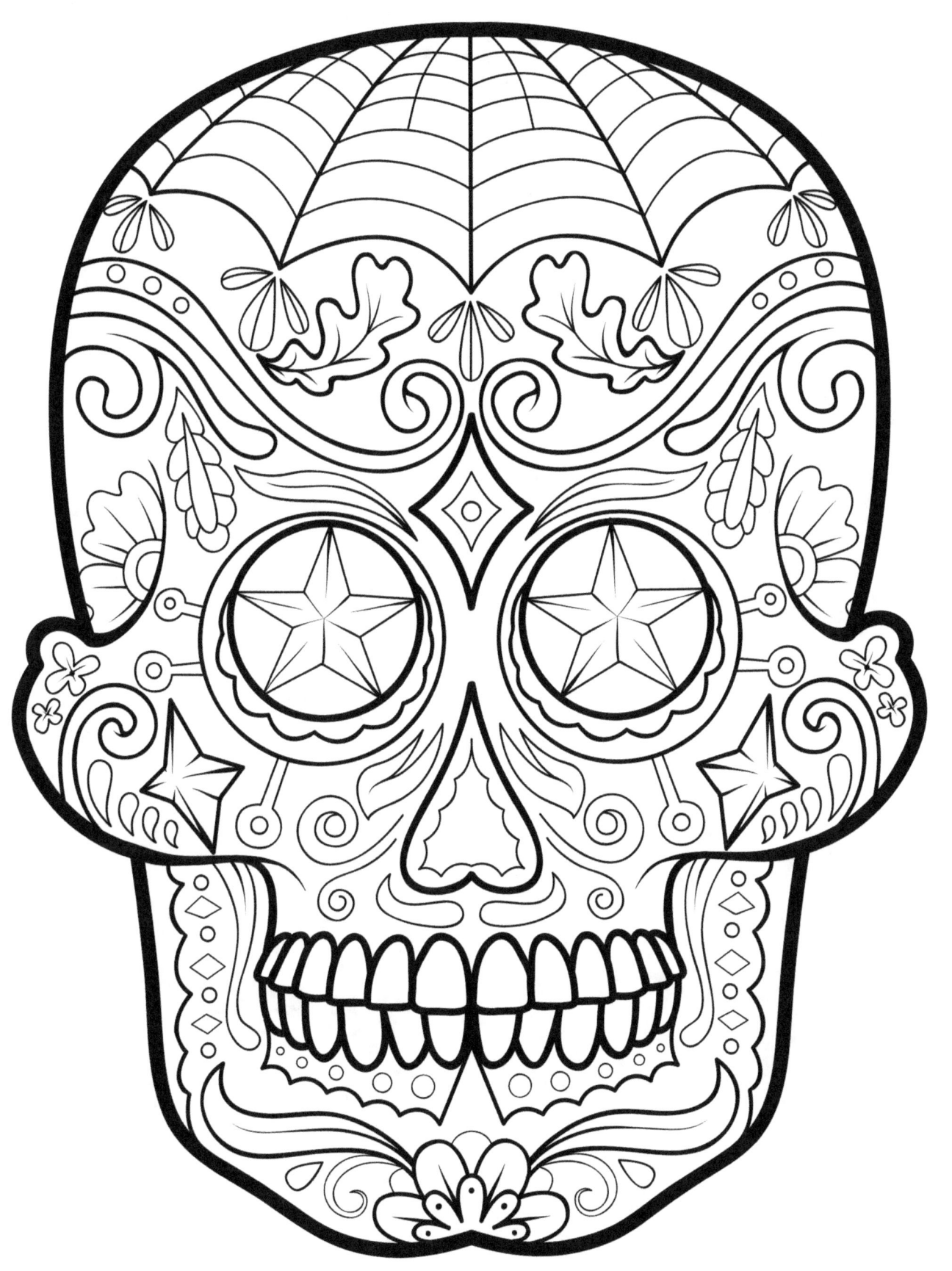

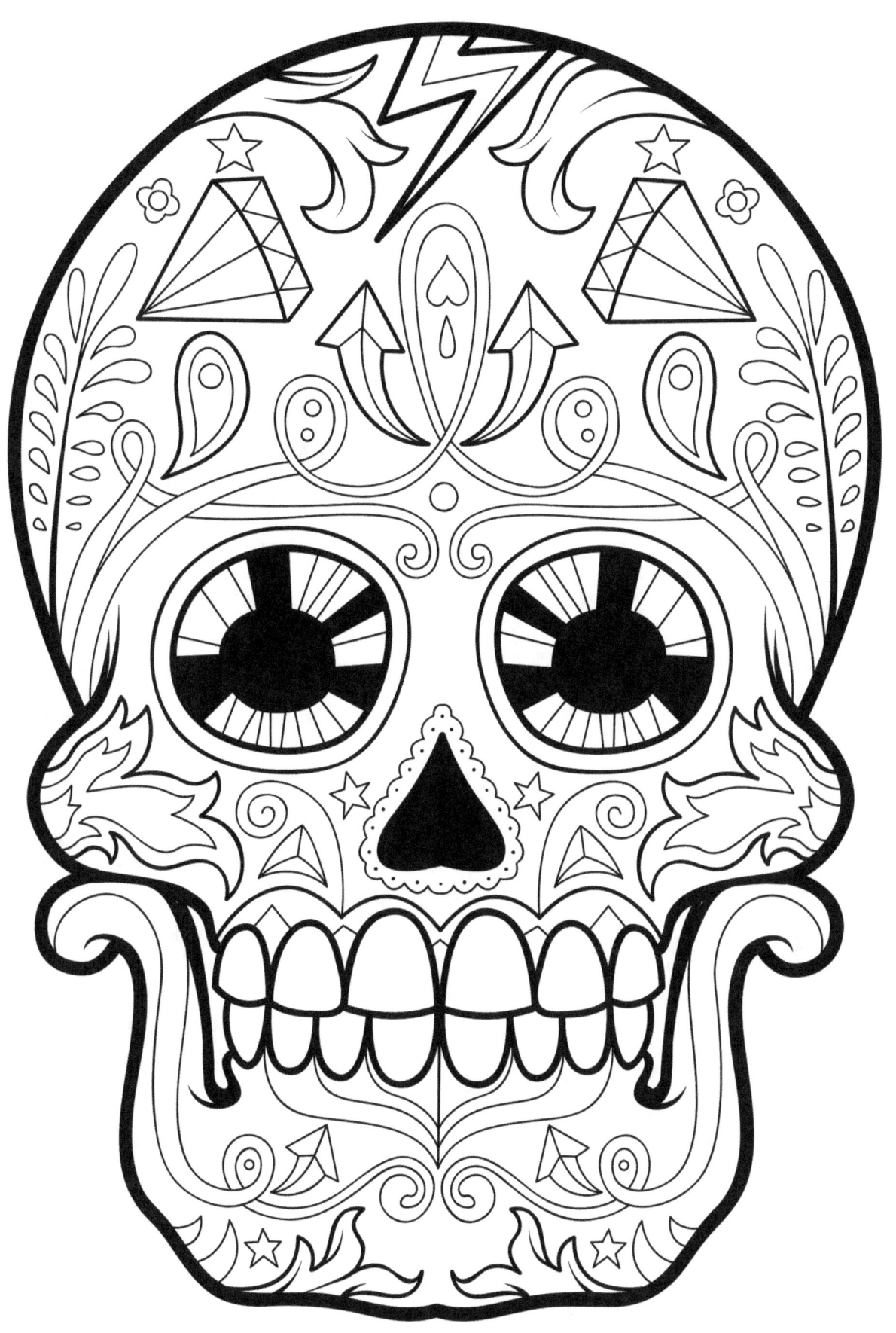

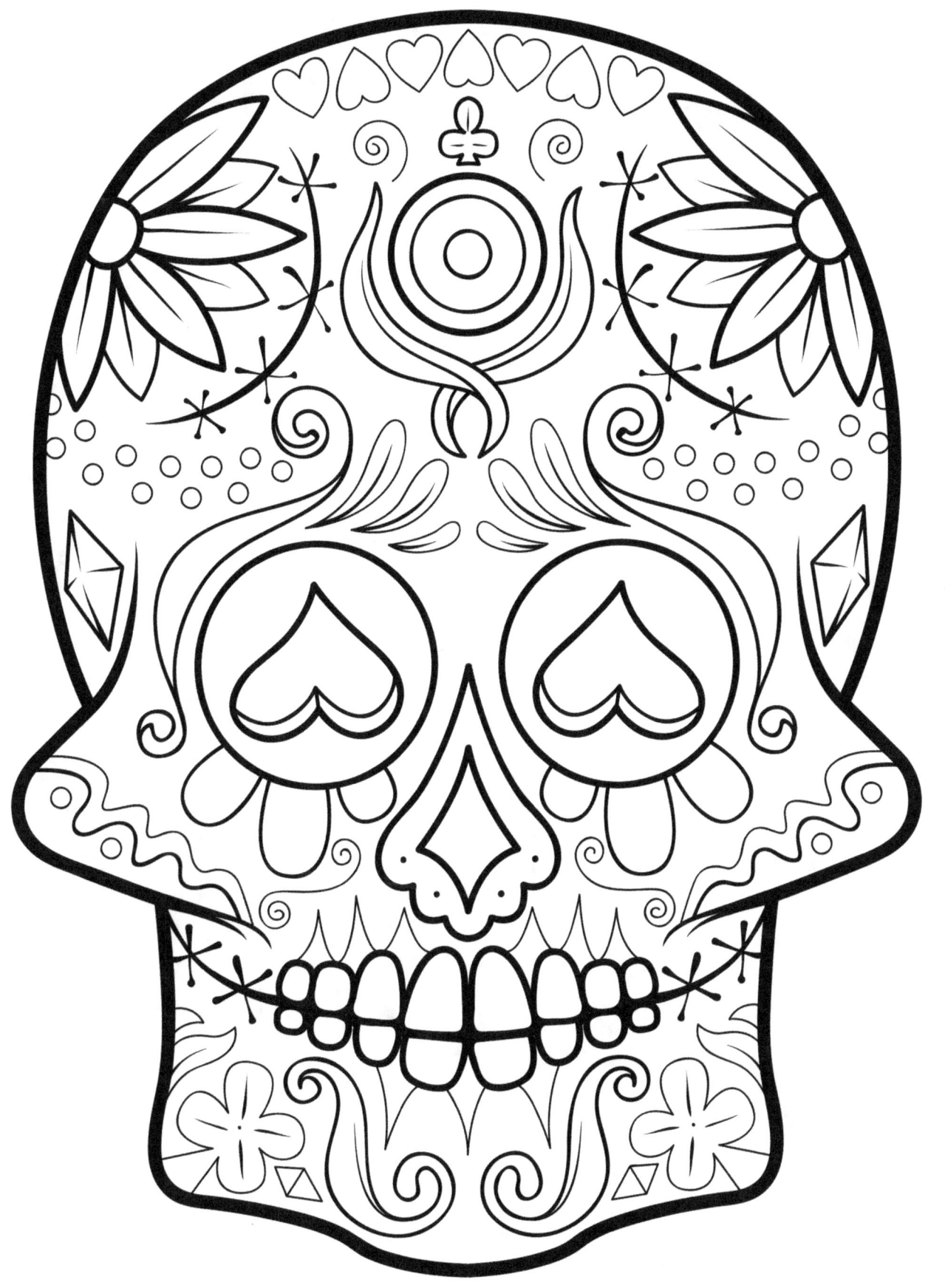

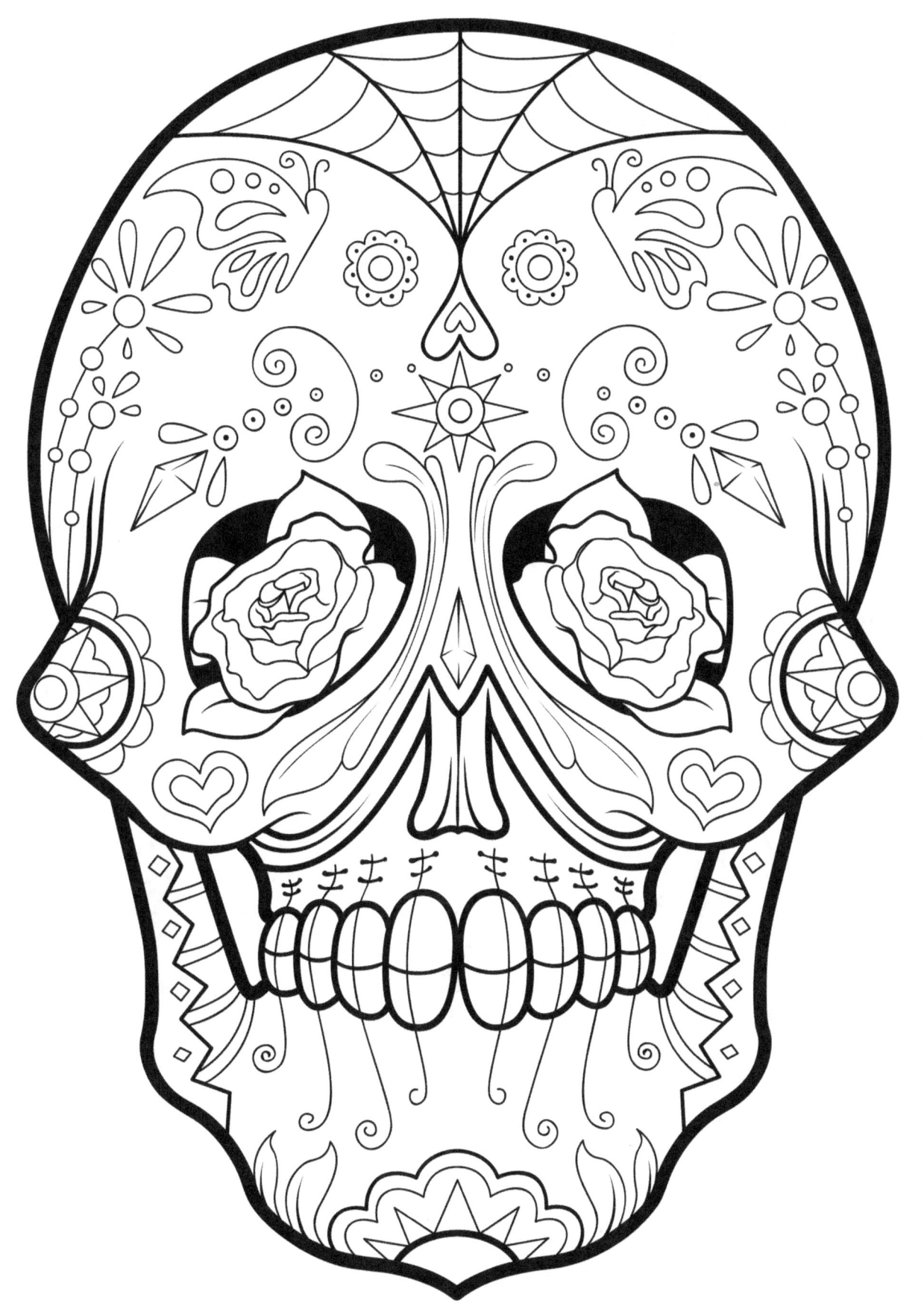

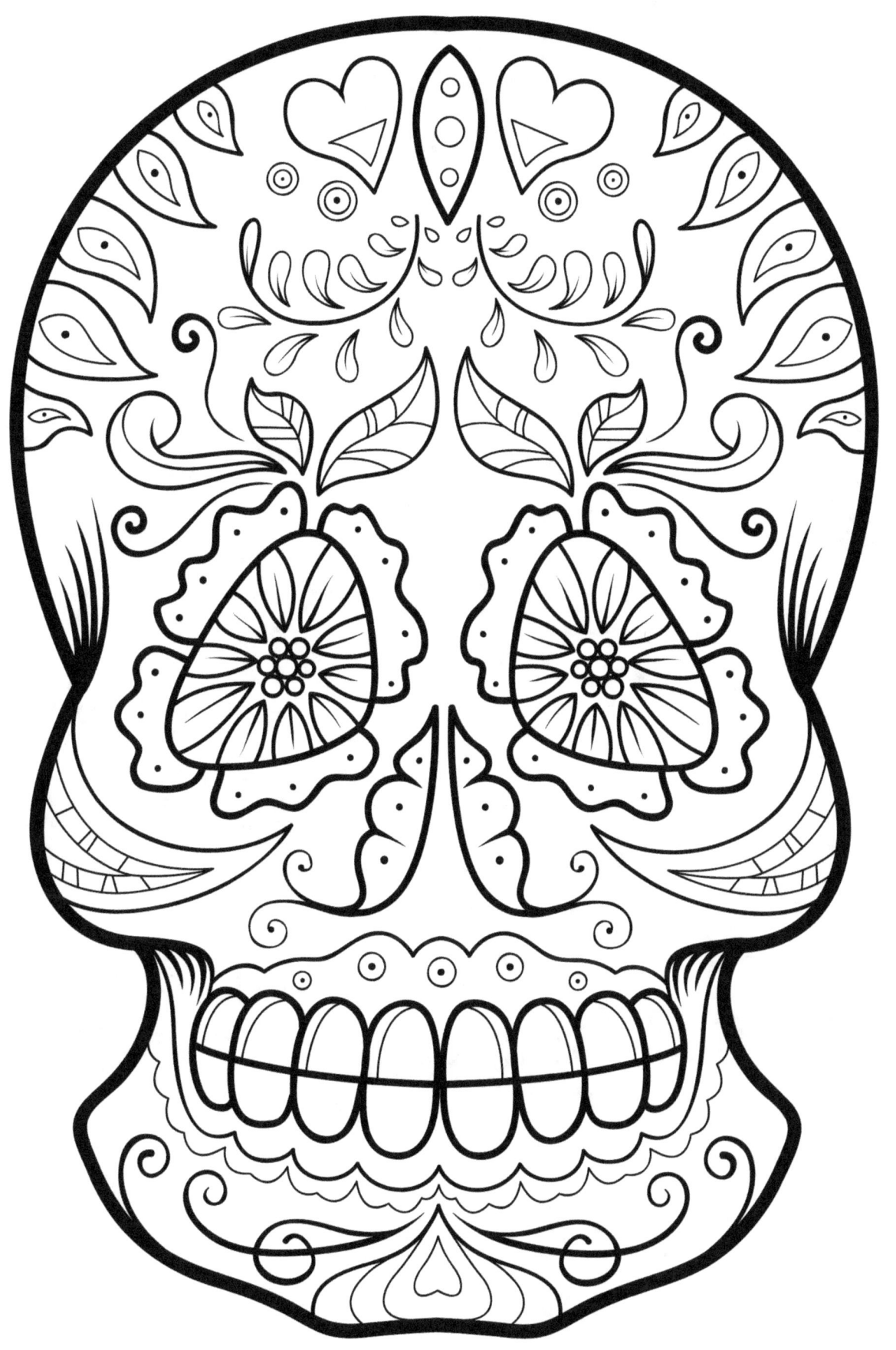

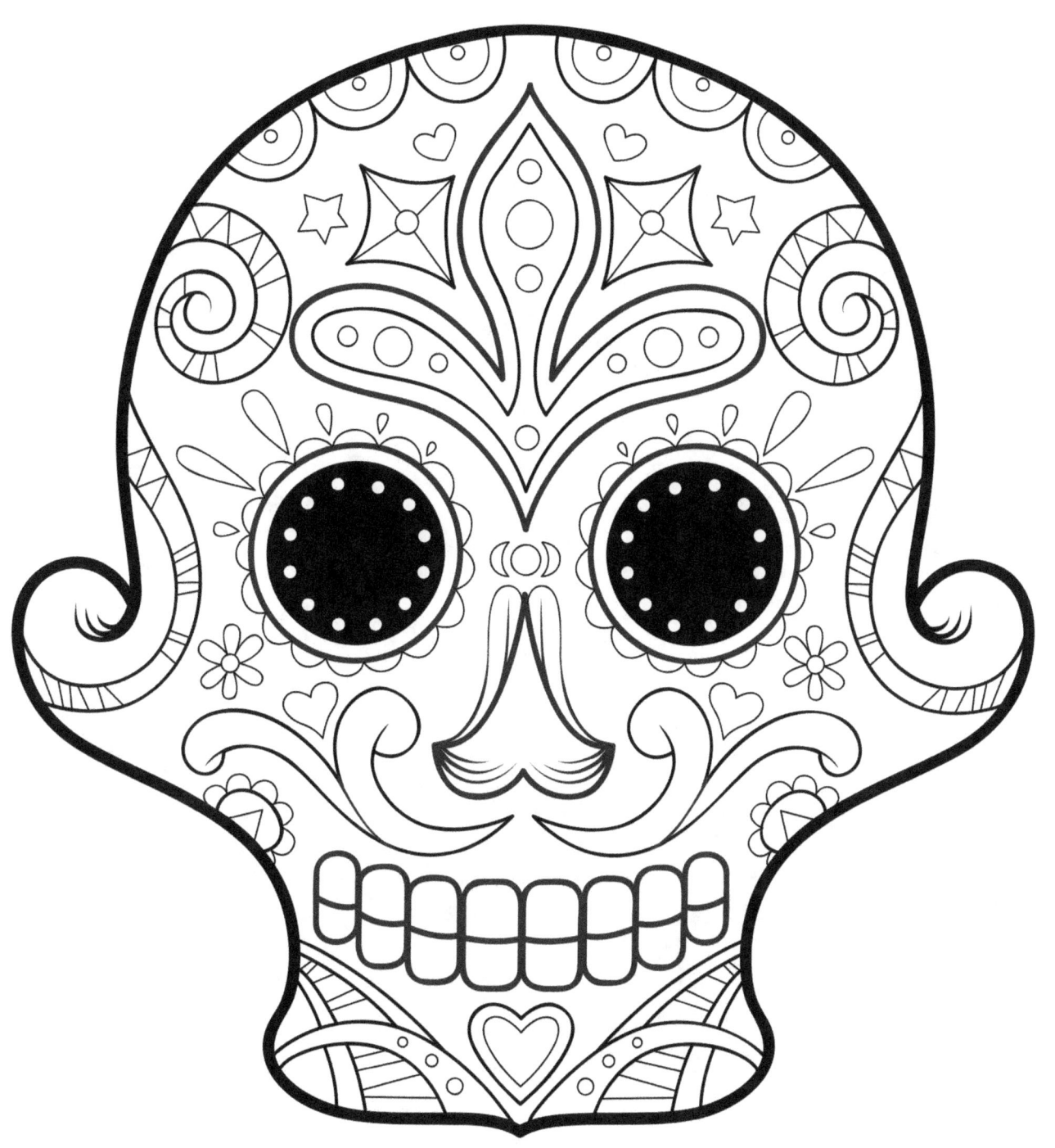

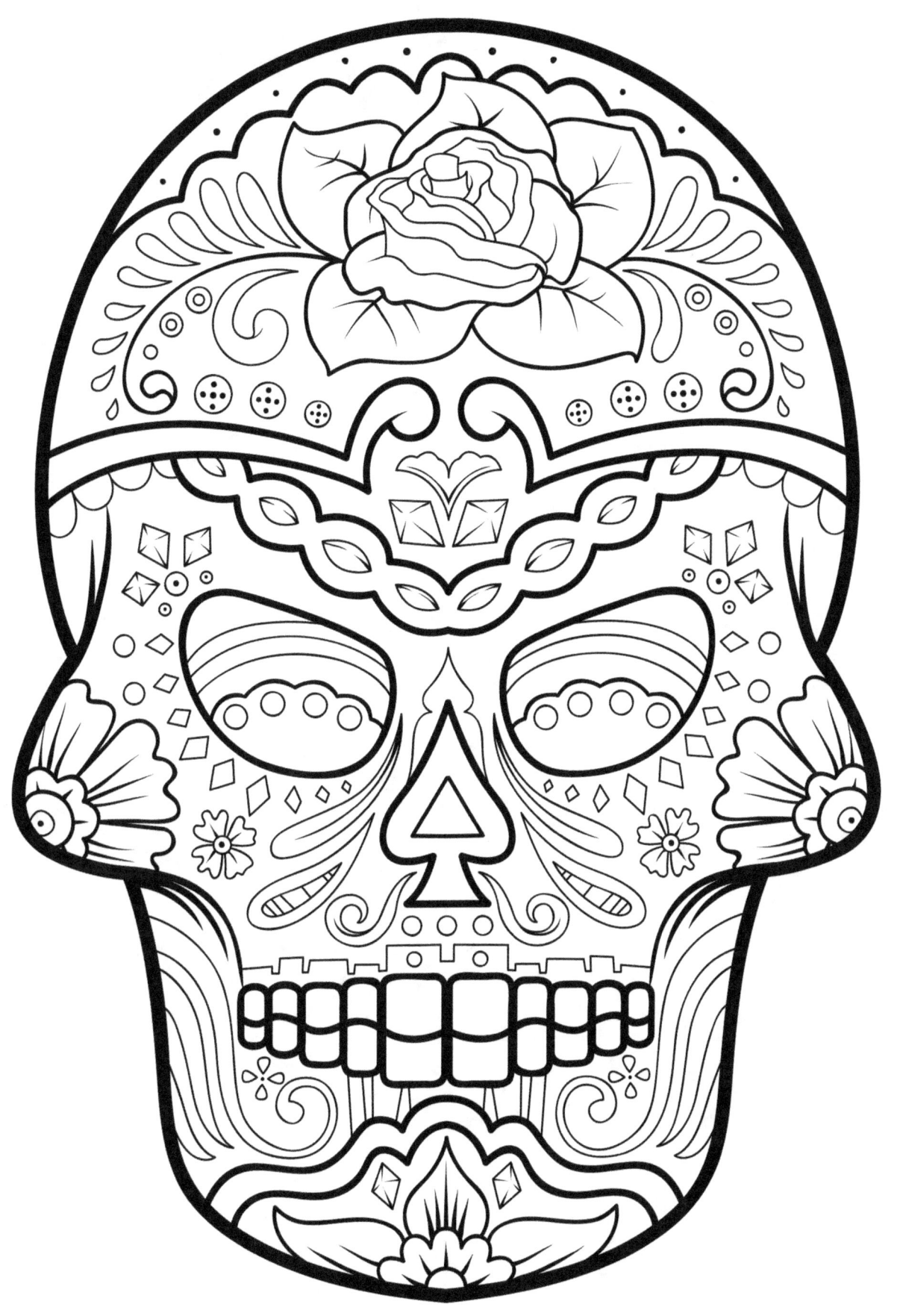

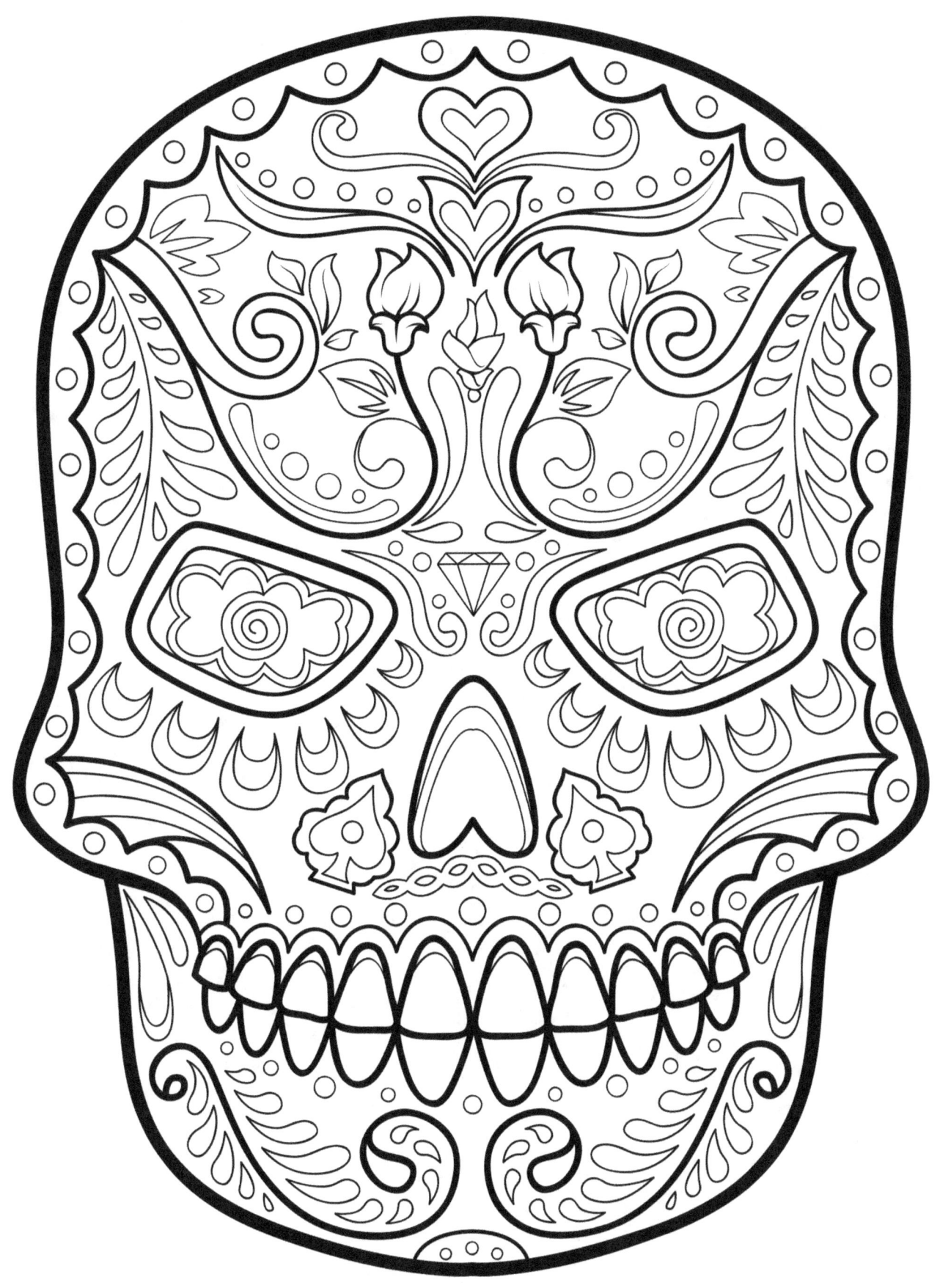

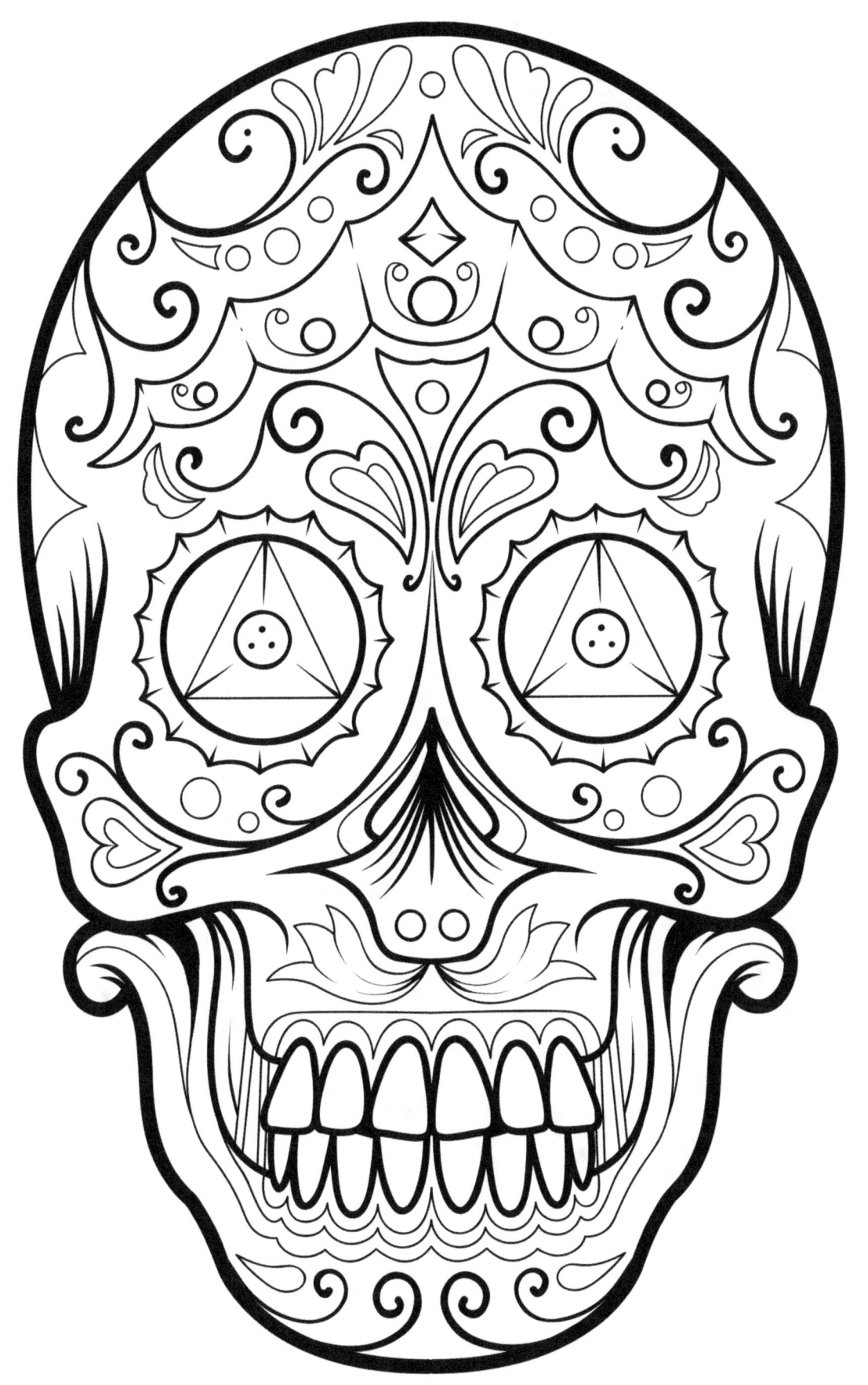

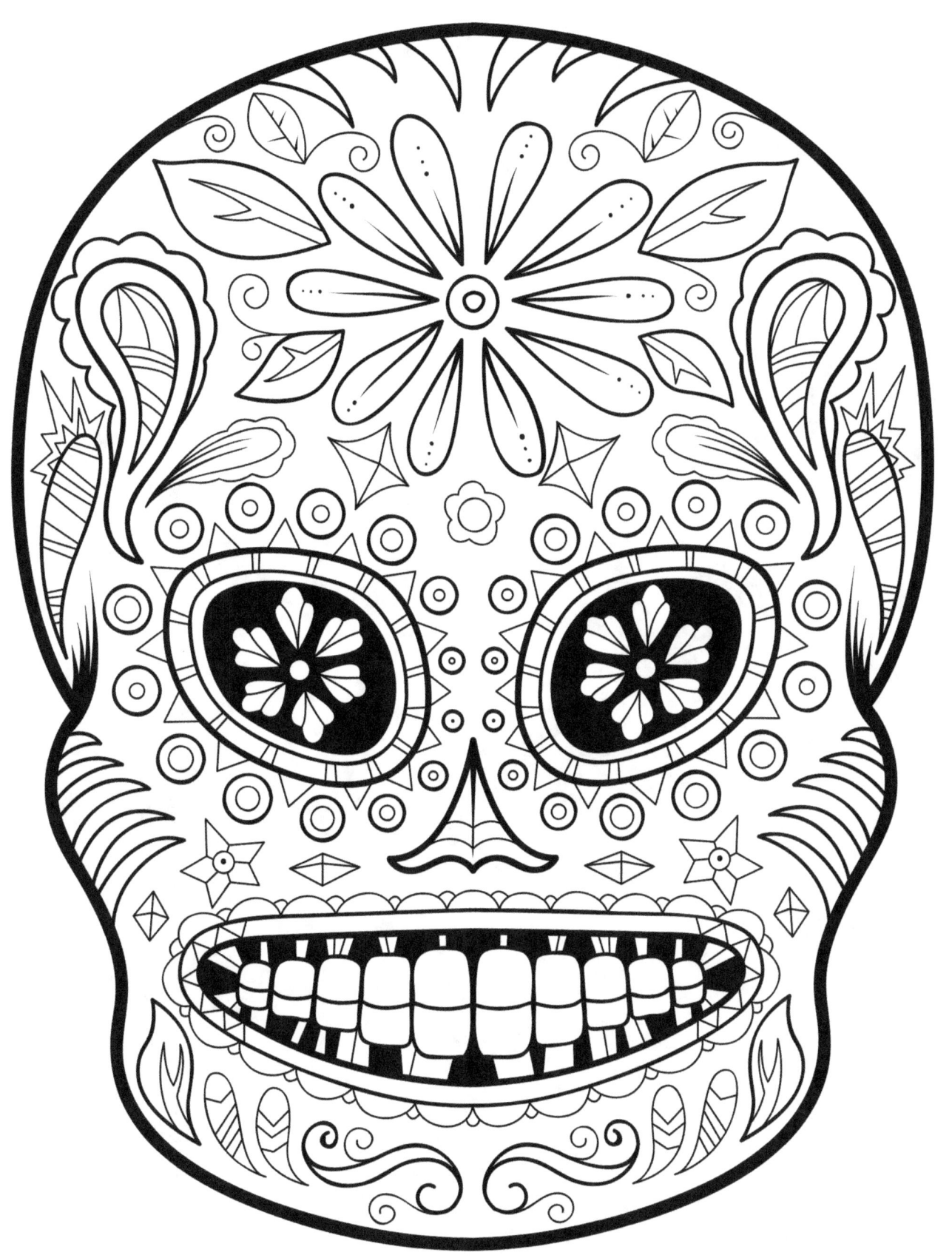

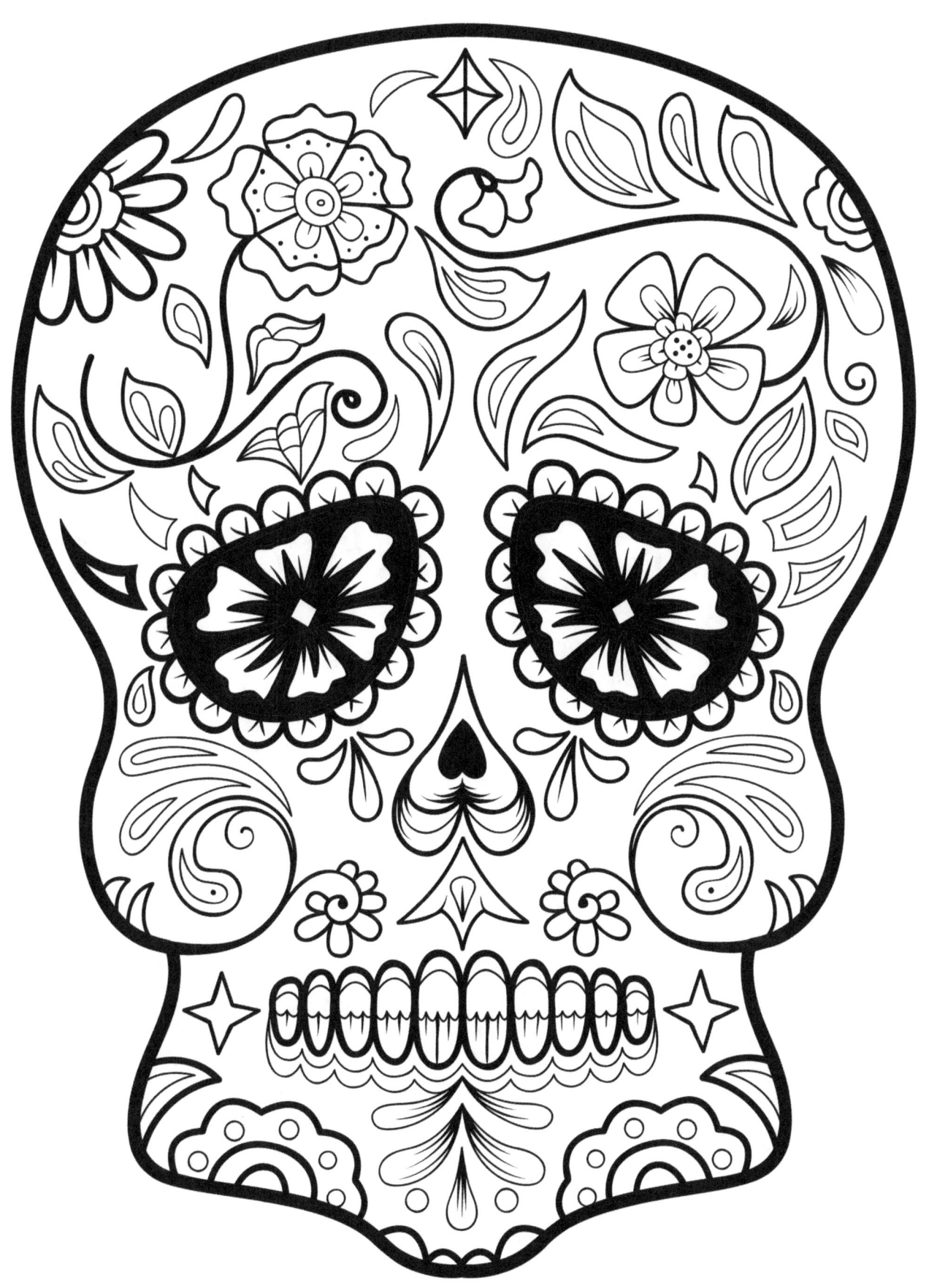

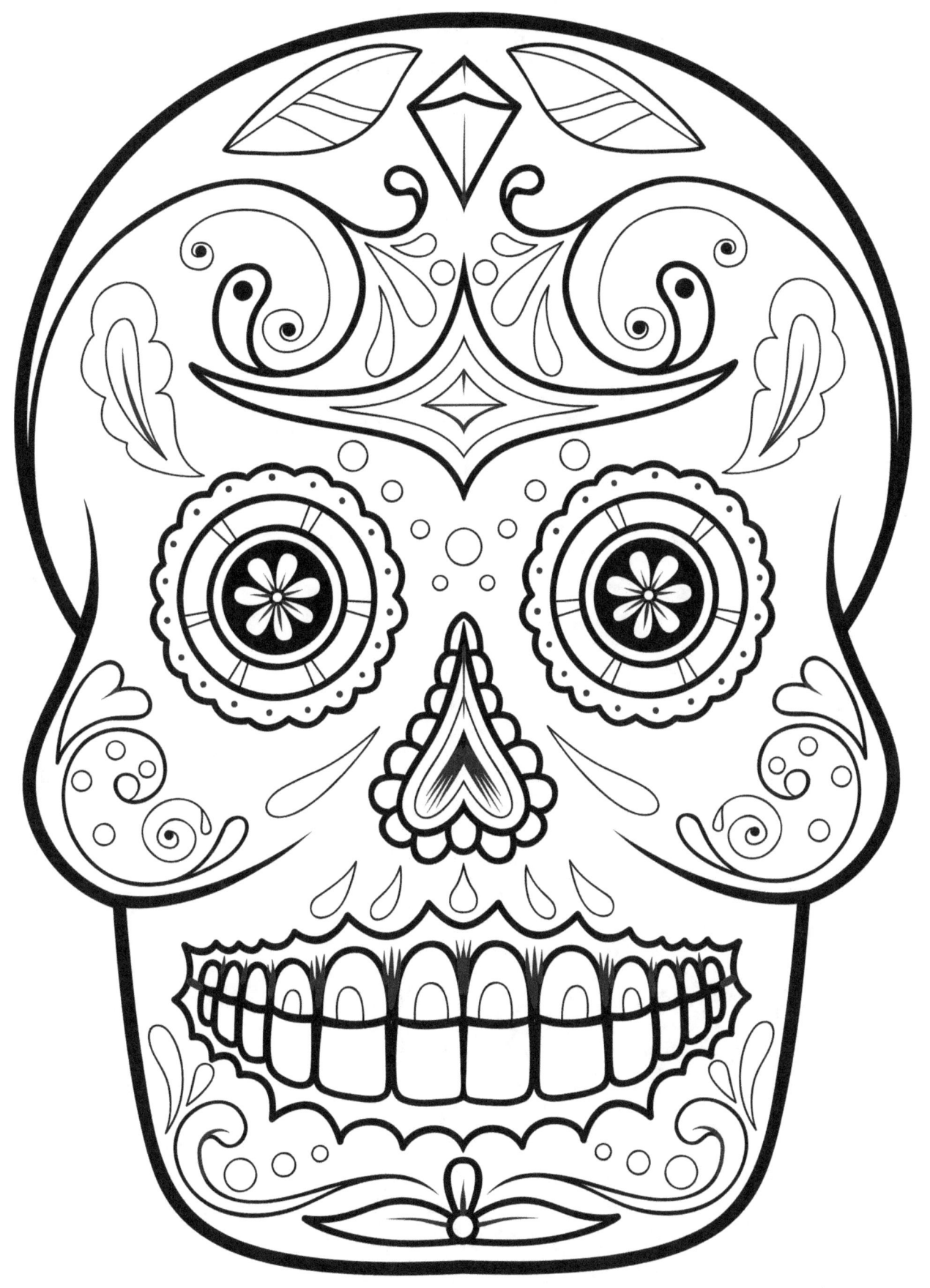

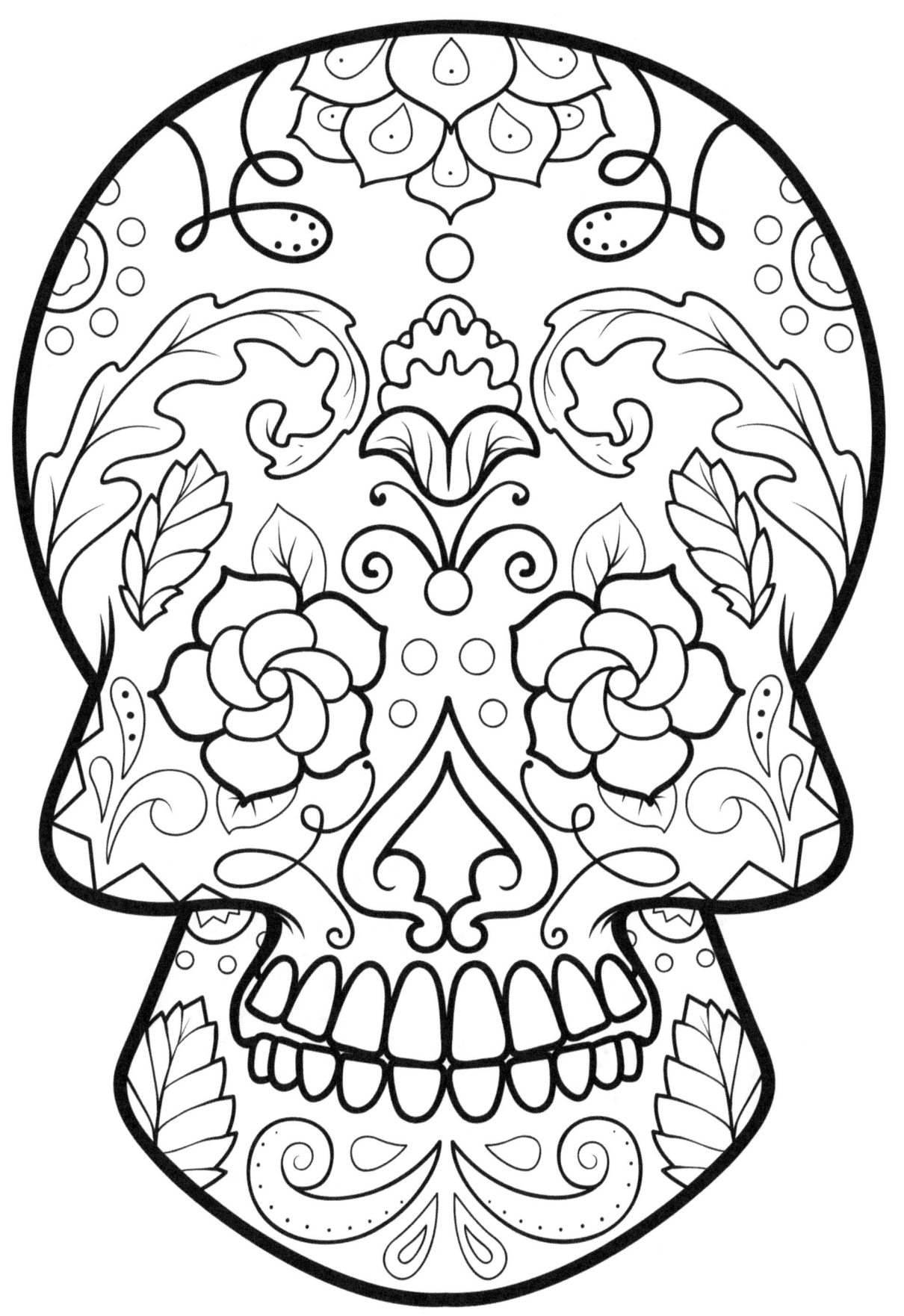

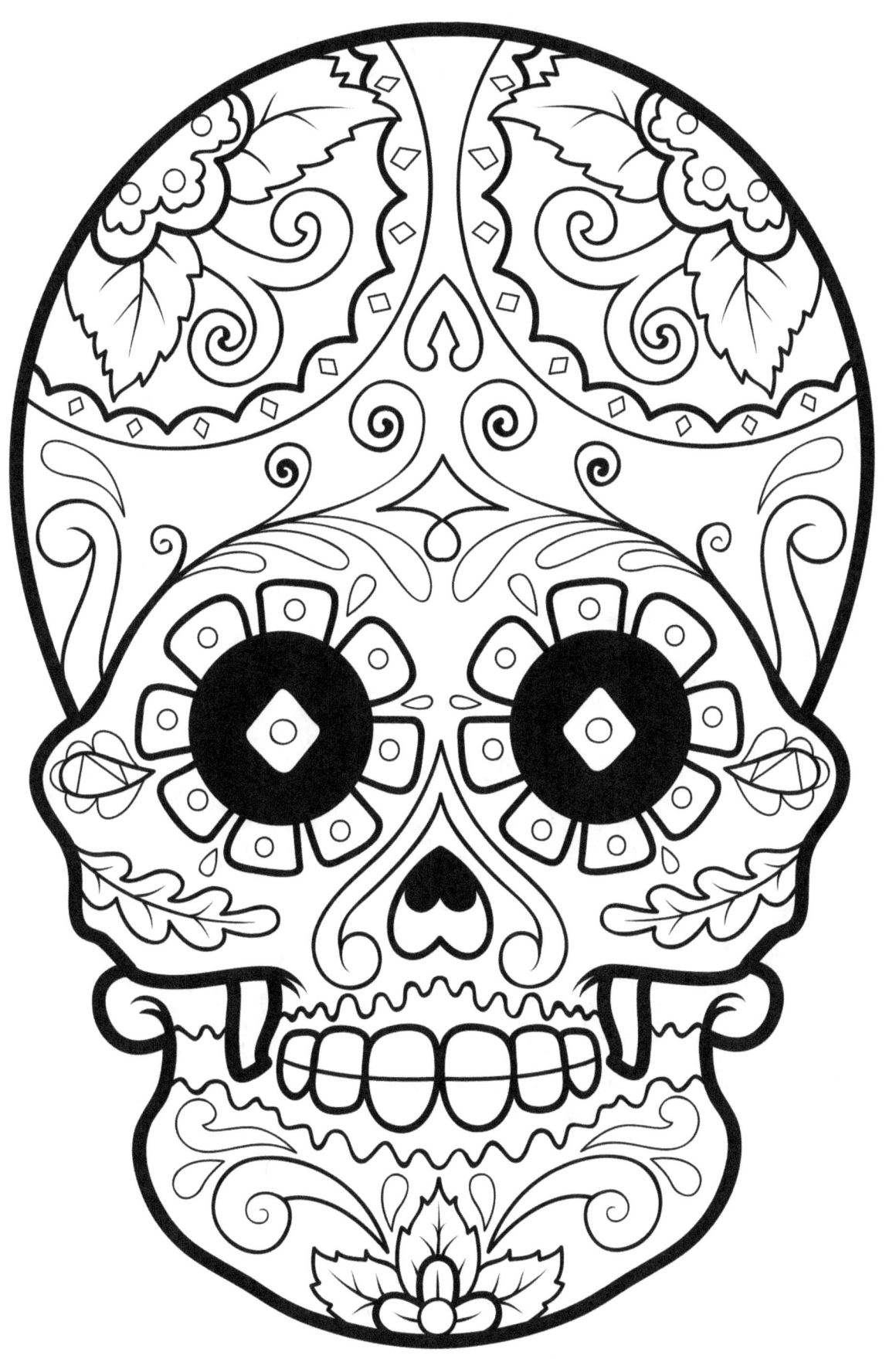

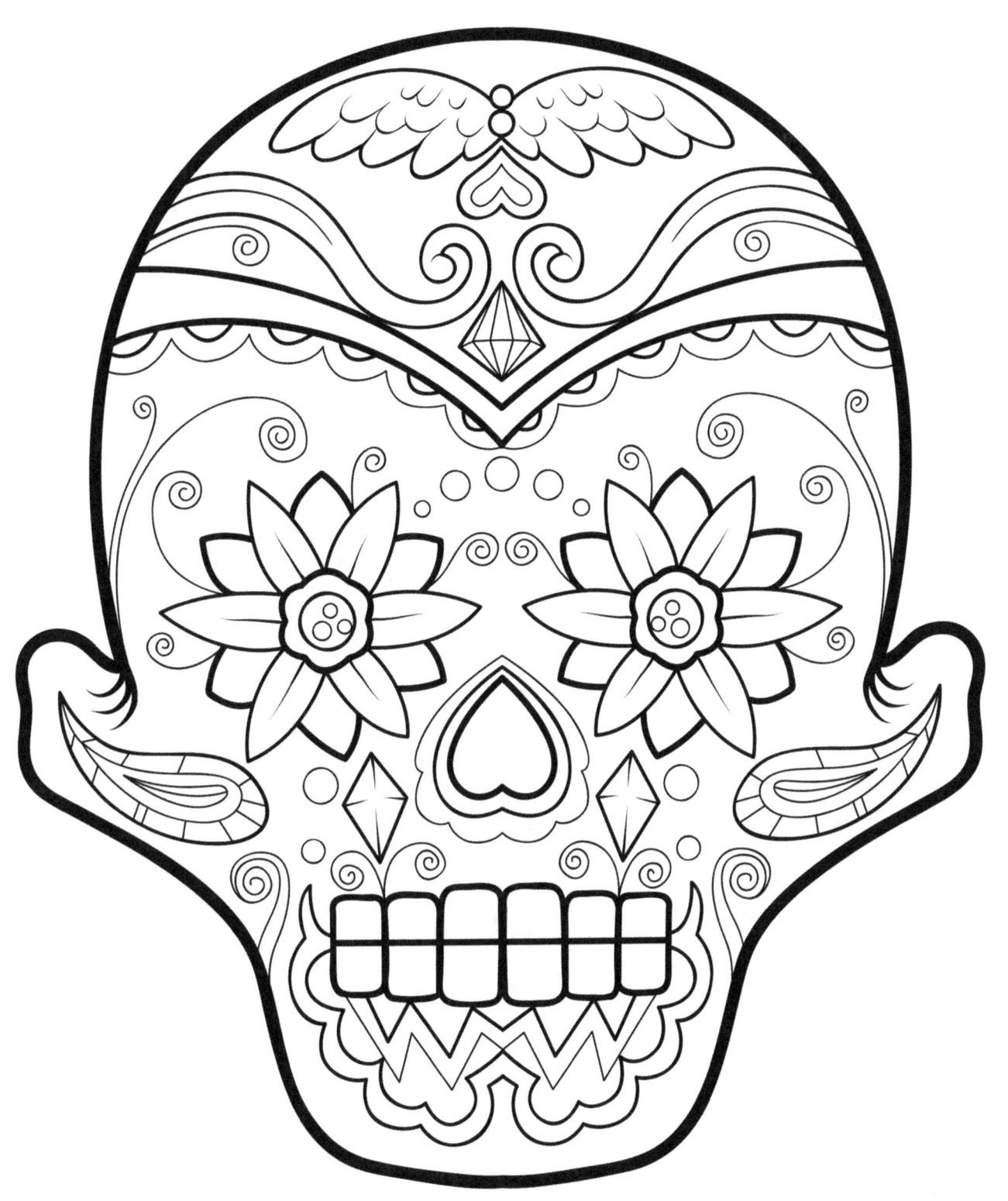

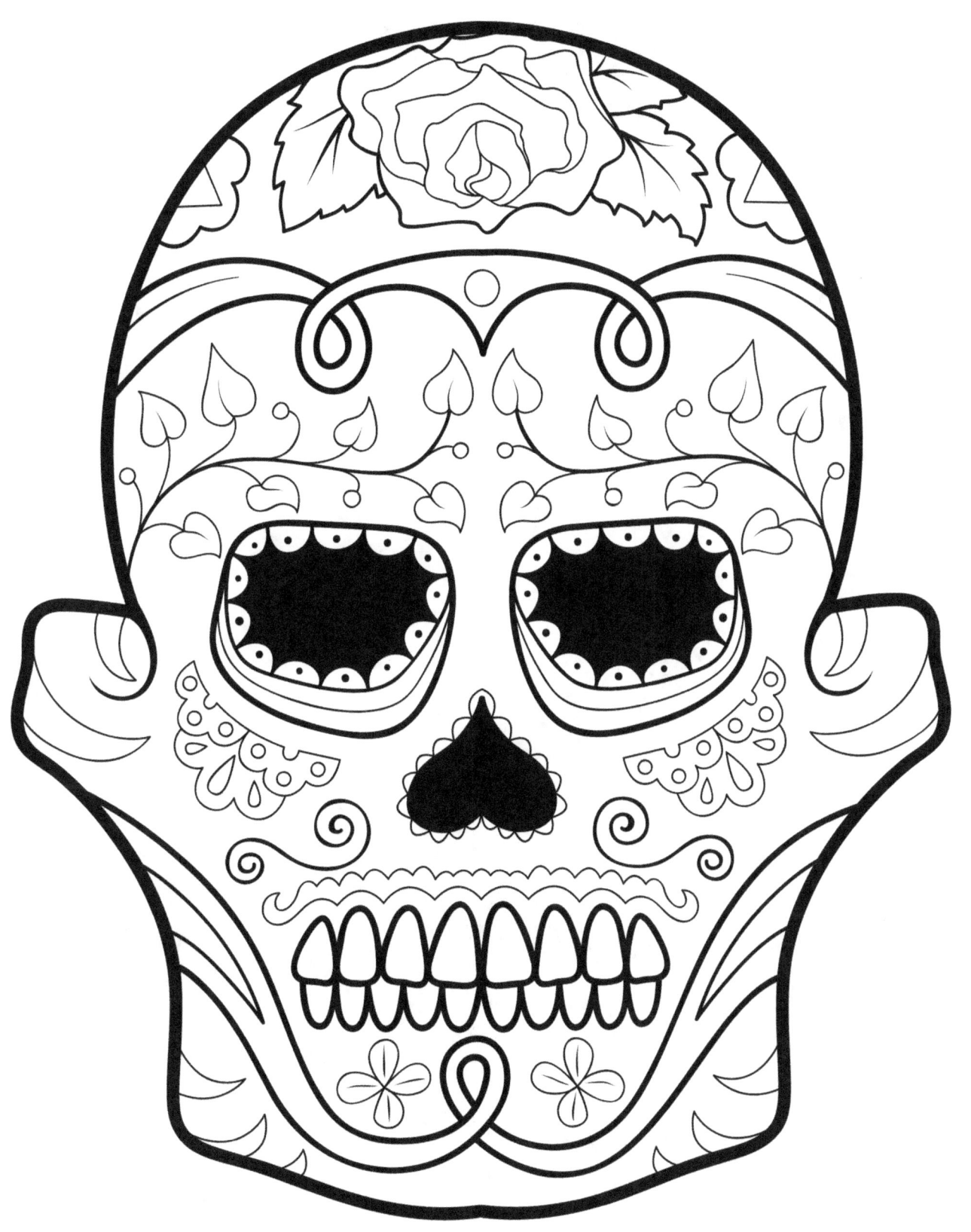

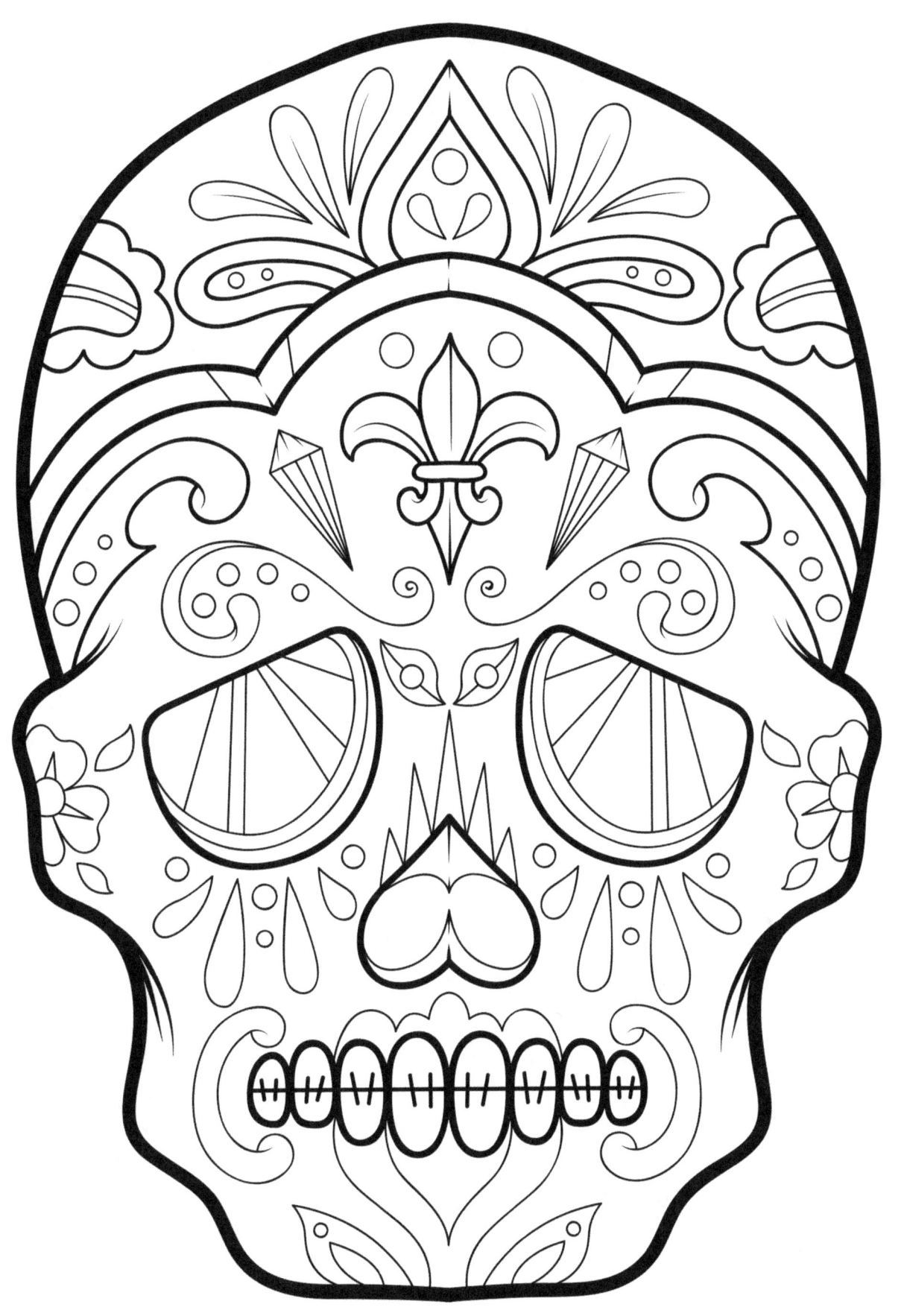

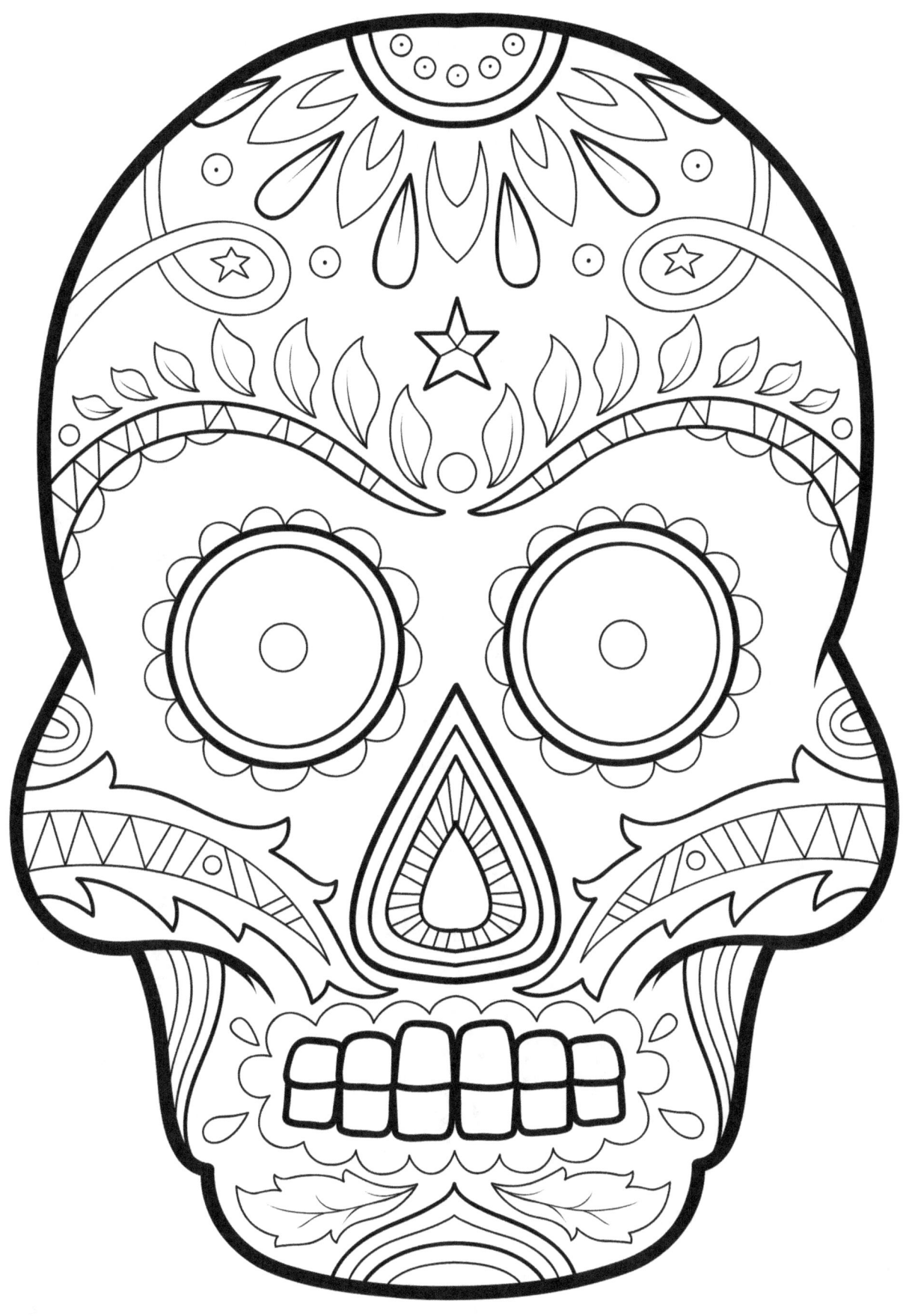

www.ingramcontent.com/pod-product-compliance
Lightning Source LLC
Chambersburg PA
CBHW081554170526
45166CB00009B/2700

* 9 7 8 1 5 1 9 4 3 6 7 5 7 *